"How do you move DEI from acronym to action? Joan Williams shines the light on the realities of the modern workplace and how small but important steps can usher in real change."

"*Bias Interrupted* could not be more valuable or more timely. As the CEO of an organization determined to come as close as we can to hiring, retaining, and benefiting from a workforce that looks like America at every level, I considered this book a godsend. It's a deeply researched blend of evidence and practical, actionable advice."

"Joan Williams's groundbreaking approaches deftly deploy leading-edge research insights across real-world organizational terrains. *Bias Interrupted* captures the pragmatic and actionable approach that enabled us to move the needle on advancing diversity and belonging."

"Professor Williams is a unicorn. A researcher, policy maker, and visionary, she offers hope for the future with a blueprint for change in the present using context from the past. This is a must-read for any leader eager to create an equitable workplace and a first-mover advantage in a post-pandemic world."

—**EVE RODSKY**, author, *Fair Play*

"Common sense. Clarity. Joan Williams brings a refreshingly actionable and necessary point of view to the poorly understood world of diversity, equity, and inclusion."

—**ABIGAIL DISNEY**, film producer, philanthropist, and social activist

"Joan Williams continues to illuminate the struggles faced by minorities and women. In a time when so many leaders are feeling helpless about how they might push the needle forward, Williams's work adds credence to the notion that small interruptions of bias can amount to big and impactful changes."

—**ERIKA V. HALL**, Associate Professor of Organization and Management, Emory University's Goizueta Business School

"This book offers a refreshingly clear-eyed view of both the problem and the solution: it is systemic and calls for rooting out the biases that beset most companies' basic business systems—biases in recruitment, hiring, and advancement that subvert our meritocratic ideals. It won't be easy, but it can be done by doggedly chipping away, step by step, with evidence-based, metrics-driven tools. This book is filled with relatable examples of these tools, how leaders can implement them, and the results they can yield."

—**ROBIN ELY,** Diane Doerge Wilson Professor of Business Administration, Harvard Business School

"Astute, pithy, and pragmatic, Joan Williams is a JEDI (Justice, Equity, Diversity, and Inclusion) warrior. Her experience and expertise shine in the chapters organized by what the C-suite and managers want to know—and need to know—to meet this pivotal moment and get it right."

—**SUSAN T. FISKE,** Eugene Higgins Professor, Psychology and Public Affairs, Princeton University

"This engaging, evidence-based book is chock-full of concrete, actionable, and research-supported steps that each of us can take to block the biases that undermine diversity and inclusion goals."

—**SHELLEY J. CORRELL,** Faculty Director, Stanford VMware Women's Leadership Innovation Lab; Michelle Mercer and Bruce Golden Family Professor of Women's Leadership, Stanford University

"A frank, straightforward discussion of how to effectively tackle diversity issues by fixing business systems, not people. Insightful, accessible, and filled with innovative solutions to seemingly intractable problems."

—**MADELINE E. HEILMAN,** Professor of Psychology, New York University

"Diversity isn't as simple as grouping together different races, genders, and cultural backgrounds. It's about building an inclusive team, with assorted thoughts and beliefs, to create a more comprehensive solution to global business issues. Even though this seems like an obvious truth, it's remarkable how seldom we apply it. By working with an inclusive team, tapping the best in each of us, building a diverse pipeline of future business leaders can be a game changer. *Bias Interrupted* is a great resource to help accelerate your DEI journey."

—**ERBY L. FOSTER JR.**, Chief Diversity Officer, The Clorox Company

"Williams gives us an accessible guide to evidence-based procedural and cultural changes organizations can make that interrupt routine biases and create real progress in diversity and inclusion. The key is careful diagnosis and consistent implementation, and she shows you how to do it."

—**CECILIA RIDGEWAY**, Lucie Stern Professor in the Social Sciences, Emerita, Stanford University

"*Bias Interrupted* is an evidence-based, data-driven, practical guide for any leader or organization that wants to move the needle on DEI. Truly a must-read!"

—**JAMES D. WHITE**, former Chair, President, and CEO, Jamba Juice

BIAS
INTERRUPTED

BIAS
INTERRUPTED

CREATING
INCLUSION
FOR REAL AND
FOR GOOD

JOAN C. WILLIAMS

HARVARD BUSINESS REVIEW PRESS
BOSTON, MASSACHUSETTS

The web addresses referenced in this book were live and correct at the time of the book's publication but may be subject to change.

Library of Congress Cataloging-in-Publication Data

Names: Williams, Joan, 1952- author.
  Title: Bias interrupted : creating inclusion for real and for good / Joan
    C. Williams.
  Description: Boston, MA : Harvard Business Review Press, [2021] |
    Includes index.
  Identifiers: LCCN 2021022672 (print) | LCCN 2021022673 (ebook) |
    ISBN 9781647822729 (paperback) | ISBN 9781647822736 (ebook)
  Subjects: LCSH: Diversity in the workplace. | Prejudices. | Equality. |
    Discrimination in employment. | Social justice. | Racism in the
    workplace.
  Classification: LCC HF5549.5.M5 W553 2021 (print) |
    LCC HF5549.5.M5 (ebook) | DDC 658.3008—dc23
  LC record available at https://lccn.loc.gov/2021022672
  LC ebook record available at https://lccn.loc.gov/2021022673
ISBN: 978-1-64782-272-9
eISBN: 978-1-64782-273-6

The paper used in this publication meets the requirements of the American National Standard for Permanence of Paper for Publications and Documents in Libraries and Archives Z39.48-1992.

To JIM

You're right, I can see gender in a ham sandwich—race and class, too.

CONTENTS

BIAS
INTERRUPTED

CHAPTER 1

What's the path forward?

"I look around me now . . . there are *no other women
engineers like me*. They just don't last. They disappear
around five years and we keep hiring and have high turnover.
I hope before I die to see some improvement."

—White woman engineer

As so often happens to me—does this happen to you?—I only
understood my real message ten years after I started saying it.*
A few weeks ago, I was listening to a health economist named
Zack Cooper on the podcast *Freakonomics*.[1] He recalled giving
a lecture to a huge insurance company, pointing out it could
save about 1 percent of its spending, roughly $1 billion, if
people got lower-limb MRI scans at the facility nearest their
homes. When he left the stage, a senior executive approached
him and said, "Hey, this is great, but we don't want research
that tells us how to save 1 percent. We want you to do the
research that tells us how to save 15 percent."

Ain't that what we all want? We want it in the diversity
arena, too. We want to go in, take a big swing, and—★ZAP★—
solve the problem.

---

*Quotations without footnotes and in italics are from my own research. Identifi-
ers have been added only where the surrounding context does not make identity
clear enough.

But it's not going to happen in diversity for the same reason it's not going to happen in health care. Too many oxen would get gored, so the politics preclude it. Too many systems would need to change, so there are too many cats to herd, cajole, persuade.

What Cooper told the executive is that there isn't one step that will save you 15 percent. What you need is a series of steps that will each save you 1 percent. Keep at it, and you will reach your goal.

This is what I knew was also true of diversity, equity, and inclusion (DEI) goals, though I'd never expressed it quite like that. We've all been looking for the grand gesture to solve the problem in one fell swoop. It doesn't exist. What does exist is a series of 1 percent changes that, with persistence, can help root out the bias that too often subverts our ideals of meritocracy.

I call these changes *bias interrupters*: evidence-based, metrics-driven tools. If a company faces diversity challenges, typically it's because bias is constantly being transmitted, day after day, through its basic business systems: the hiring process, performance evaluations, the way access is granted to valued opportunities.

In the wake of Black Lives Matter and the national reckoning with racism in the United States,[2] we are finally beginning to understand that, to address systemic racism, you have to change systems. That's the only way to fix policing. It's the only way to fix companies, too.

Think about it—if your company had a problem with sales, you would not try to fix it by holding deep, sincere conversations about how much everyone values sales. You would not develop programming for Celebrate Sales Month.

You would use basic business tools: evidence about what's going wrong, and metrics to measure your progress in fixing it. We need to tackle DEI using the same tools. I suspect this will come as a relief to the many CEOs who feel more comfortable solving business problems than leading earnest conversations about the inner workings of social inequality. And it will come as a relief to the CFOs who are fed up with spending billions on DEI efforts with remarkably few results.

No wonder CFOs are frustrated. The basic tools of the diversity industrial complex don't work. Employee resource groups and mentoring programs for women and people of color are useful in creating a sense of community and support for those who feel isolated in organizations. But we need to stop focusing nigh exclusively on helping people navigate systems that remain fundamentally unfair. We need to change the systems.

The other basic tool of the diversity industrial complex is bias training. These sessions don't work for a very simple reason: you can't change a culture by doing anything just once, or once a year. To make matters worse, too often companies have relied on bias trainings that were ineffective or even counterproductive.[3] Many early sensitivity-type trainings just weren't very good. For example, many of these sessions defined diversity to include anything and everything: attractiveness, weight, personality type, smoking. This blurred the real issue, which is whether well-documented forms of social inequality are shaping workplaces in ways that jeopardize meritocracy.

The newer generation of trainings also often fall short. Many of these are based on the widely used Implicit Association Test (IAT). IAT-based trainings are an improvement on sensitivity training, since they signal that diversity efforts must be based on rigorous evidence, which IAT seeks to collect. But IAT-based trainings too often focus on the cognitive bases of bias. For example, one video instructs viewers to watch people passing a basketball around. Often participants are so intent on counting the number of passes that they fail to notice a large man in a gorilla suit striding across the basketball court.[4] The video is a great way to highlight that human beings are designed to pay selective attention to certain things while tuning out a lot more. But what's the takeaway? Look for gorillas?

This book uses a different approach that is still evidence-based. Instead of focusing on people's subconscious thoughts, I like to look at how people actually behave.

Consider matched-résumé studies, in which researchers use résumés that are identical but for one factor to see how likely each candidate is to get a job interview, promotion, etc. By eliminating every difference except for race or sex, these studies provide objective evidence that bias drives decision making.

One of my favorites is a study where researchers responded to over 1,300 employment ads and found that a candidate named Jamal typically needed eight additional years of experience to get the same number of job callbacks as a candidate named Greg—who, again, had an otherwise identical résumé.[5]

Another favorite study sent 1,276 job applications, using the identical résumés of two women—the only difference being that one listed her membership in the parent-teacher association. The mother was half as likely to get called back for an interview.[6] The researchers found similar results in a lab experiment in which they asked volunteers to rate the identical résumés on a number of factors. The results showed that mothers were seen as less competent and committed, less worthy of promotion, and less suitable for management. They were also held to stricter performance and punctuality standards than childless women and were offered $11,000 less in salary.

As with this study, most matched-résumé studies don't involve real job applicants. Do these studies actually describe what goes on at work? My research over the past ten years, surveying people across diverse industries and actual workplaces, shows they do.

At the Center for WorkLife Law, my team invented a simple survey that picks up bias based on race, gender, social class origin, and age. We call it the Workplace Experiences Survey (WES).* (This chapter's epigraph comes from a respondent to that survey.) In fourteen studies of nearly 18,000 people in different industries and organizations over nearly a decade, we consistently found the same five patterns of bias. These are described in much more detail in one of my prior

---

*When I describe the results of our studies, for simplicity I say, for example, "engineers" rather than "respondents to our survey." See the appendix for details.

books, *What Works for Women at Work*,[7] and in WorkLife Law reports on gender and racial bias in academia, engineering, architecture, and tech in the United States and in engineering in India.[8]

Inclusion is the right goal, but it's too vague to be actionable. WES data pins down the jellyfish often described as "lack of inclusion" in a one-hundred-question, ten-minute survey, to make bias visible to those not affected by it. Here's what bias looks like on the ground, with verbatim responses from my research.

- **Prove-it-again bias means some groups have to prove themselves more than others.** White men from college-educated families tend to be judged on potential, while groups less privileged by race, class, or gender are judged on performance.* *"Others are judged on potential. I have always—always—had to show demonstrated results,"* said a Black former CEO. Among architects, about half of women and people of color, but only a quarter of white men, report having to prove themselves more than their colleagues; this pattern repeats in other professions. Thus the African American adage "You have to be twice as good to get half as much."

- **Tightrope bias means some groups need to be politically savvier than others to succeed.** Typically, white men

---

*For readability, I will not repeat "tend to be" every time I make a statement about a group. Keep in mind that all generalizations about groups reflect tendencies, not absolutes.

can be authoritative and ambitious—two highly valued workplace traits—but women walk a tightrope: they risk being seen as abrasive if they are authoritative and unqualified if they aren't. "So if you're stern . . . or you say no, the immediate reaction is to call that woman a bitch, right? If you're a man, it's just a no." People of color who behave assertively may well be seen as "angry" if they're Black, "feisty" if they're Latina, or "untrustworthy" if they're Asian American. "You have to avoid the stereotype of the 'angry Black female,' which diminishes your opinion and the weight of your argument," said a statistician. In engineering, only half of women and people of color, but over two-thirds of white men, said they could behave assertively without pushback.[9]

- *Tug-of-war bias* **reflects that bias against a group can fuel conflict within that group.** White men from college-educated families typically benefit from in-group favoritism, but it can be politically costly for other groups to support their own in-group. *"A coworker made chauvinistic comments at another coworker, and I did not have the courage at the time to speak up for her,"* said a white woman.

- *Racial stereotypes* **further disadvantage people of color.** For example, Asian Americans are seen as a great match for technical work but lacking in leadership potential. *"As an Asian American man, I often felt firm leadership would overlook my leadership contributions and*

*capabilities."** Black professionals report high levels
of social isolation and startling forms of disrespect.
*"Isolation . . . you don't know who you can trust . . . and
alienating—this has been a very lonely life."* Latinx professionals may be written off as "angry" for behavior
that, in a white man, would be seen as a career-
enhancing passion for the business. *"I wasn't angry.
I just wasn't deferential."*

- **Maternal wall bias—bias against mothers—is the strongest form of gender bias.** Women who become mothers
  often face assumptions that they are less competent
  (think "pregnancy brain") and less committed—and in
  fact *shouldn't* be as committed to their careers now that
  they have a kid. *"I took leave after having a child, and when
  I returned there was no longer meaningful work for me at the
  firm."* Though 80 percent of white male lawyers said
  that having children didn't sink their perceived competence, only 44 percent of white women said the same.[10]

These five forms of bias have obvious negative effects
on people who experience them. Our data from the WES
shows that they hurt companies, too. Increases in bias are
linked with decreases in ability to do one's best work, intent
to stay, ability to see a path for advancement, belonging, and
career satisfaction.

---

*Our surveys sometimes use the category "Asian Americans," sometimes "people
of Asian descent" (which includes immigrants). I use the terms interchangeably
for readability. For brevity, some figures use the abbreviation "API women" or
"API men."

You can't change what you can't see. This book is designed to help by making bias visible.

The conjunction of WES data and decades of lab studies is much more powerful than either data set alone. Lab studies provide an objective measure to show that bias exists in the world. The Workplace Experiences Survey is an attitudinal study that shows that bias patterns that exist in the world are also reported in the workplace.

Throughout this book you will see charts that represent answers to questions from the Workplace Experiences Survey. The values represent the percentage of people who agreed with the statement in the chart. The data comes from individual organizations as well as national samples from different professions—architecture, engineering, law, academia, and tech. For the most part, results were similar between professions. Typically, we report results for white men, white women, women of color, and men of color, although in two data sets we have data only on women, and for one data set the representation of men of color was too low to be useful. In addition, where available and relevant, we have pinpointed the specific group whose experience diverged most sharply from the experience of white men (typically, this is a subgroup of women of color). This data was collected between 2014 and 2020. In some surveys there were slight differences in question wording and demographic groupings.

While the data these charts come from is comprehensive, the charts themselves provide snapshots—a way to understand the statistics that's more accessible than burying the data in sentences. (Reading statistics is a slog compared to seeing them.) The charts highlight the major points and provide a visual exclamation point to the idea that pervasive bias needs interrupting.

Another aspect of pinning down the jellyfish is pinpointing how bias plays out in organizational systems. Our data documents how bias affects a wide range of workplace processes, including hiring, performance evaluations, assignments, sponsorship, pay, promotions, and compensation.[11] White men are (often dramatically) more likely than other groups to report that workplace systems are fair, as figure 1-1 shows.[12] For example, in engineering, women of color are thirty-two percentage points less likely than white men to feel they have access to desirable assignments; Black women are thirty percentage points less likely than white men to think pay is fair.

Many prior studies have documented bias in hiring, performance evaluations, and pay.[13] One meta-analysis found that differences between men and women in salary, bonuses, promotions, and other rewards were fourteen times larger than the differences in performance evaluations.[14] That means that for women, a good performance evaluation is much less likely to turn into a raise or promotion.

The Workplace Experiences Survey also documents that many of the biases that negatively affect people of color also affect women (regardless of race) and first-generation professionals (regardless of gender). Because women of color face at least two powerful kinds of bias, we find in industry after industry that they typically report the highest levels of

FIGURE 1-1

White men, more than any other group, see workplace systems as fair

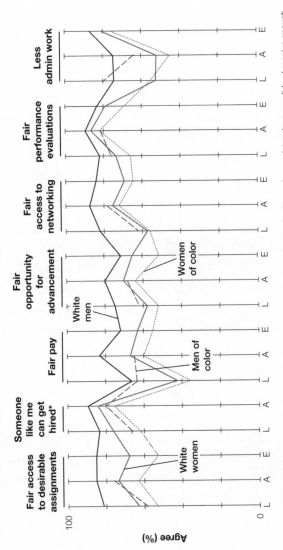

Note: L = lawyers, A = architects, and E = engineers. The lines in the graph for male engineers of color are incomplete where we did not receive enough responses from them to draw conclusions.

*This statement wasn't included in the survey for engineers.

many kinds of bias. That's why so many of the quotes in this book are from women of color: it's an economical way to describe the experience of both women and people of color.

Here's the bottom line: race, gender, and class privilege converge to create very different workplace conditions for white men than for any other group. White men report dramatically lower rates of each pattern of bias than other groups in almost every case, as figure 1-2 shows.

The large differences between white men and other groups are all the more significant because small amounts of bias can have big effects. One study used a mathematical model to see what would happen if there were only a 5 percent gender bias in performance ratings—a much smaller level of bias than exists in many companies today. After eight rounds of promotions, an organization that started out 58 percent women would be only 29 percent women.[15] Another study found that small amounts of gender bias in law firm performance evaluations made it nearly three times more likely that men would be promoted to partner.[16] Like interest, bias compounds.

Because white men remain overrepresented at the top of most organizations, they are often the people in charge of solving DEI problems. But if they're not seeing those problems, they may feel like they are flying blind. Again, you can't change what you can't see.

Although at most companies, the in-group is composed chiefly of white men, not all white men are in the in-group, because not all of them have the same experience. In particular, the experience of professionals who are first-generation

FIGURE 1-2

White men are are less likely than any other group to report bias

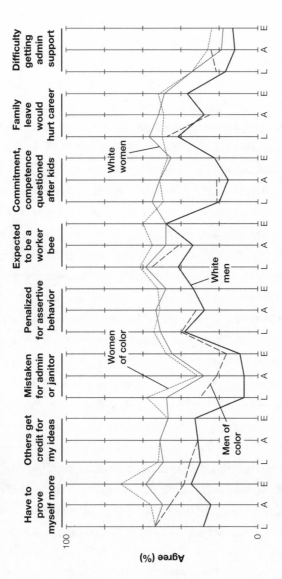

Note: L = lawyers, A = architects, and E = engineers. The lines in the graph for male engineers of color are incomplete where we did not receive enough responses from them to draw conclusions.

(first-gen) college graduates differs from that of profession-als from college-educated families. First-gen professionals, including white men, report more bias and lower levels of belonging, though this varies a lot by industry.* Our data suggests it's far stronger in industries like law and real estate investing, which depend greatly on socializing and cultural capital, than in industries like engineering, which depend chiefly on technical knowledge.

All this helps to explain why there's been so little prog-ress on diversity. The problem is much bigger and more en-trenched than trainings or mentoring programs can solve. Too often, companies have hoped for a quick and easy fix. Or they have hired people of color or women, only to lose them over and over again because these employees find they can't do their best work or advance at a fair pace.

The good news is many of those 1 percent interventions are ready to be used. Bias *can* be interrupted; it's not as im-possible as it may seem. And interrupting bias improves the workplace experience for everyone: people of color, women—and also white men.[17] White men (along with everyone else) get concrete benefits like more-constructive feedback, a better "fit" with workplace culture, and less flak for having personal or family responsibilities. They also gain the satisfaction of knowing they work in a true meritocracy.

You can't boil the ocean, so where to start? Our research and experience shows that the best first step is to interrupt

---

*When I use the term "first-generation professional" or "first-gen," I mean people in professional-managerial jobs from families where neither parent went to college.

bias in systems like hiring, assignments, performance evaluations, and promotions. But few DEI efforts set out to do
this systematically. Small steps can produce big changes if
those steps are evidence-based and suited to your company
culture. Improving the quality of business systems helps the
business.

This book offers a cutting-edge, objective, relentless approach to interrupting bias. The problem is real, but so is
the solution.

- Chapter 2 examines the debate over whether bias
  training is worthless.

- Chapters 3 and 4 discuss the two most prevalent
  forms of racial and gender bias, explaining how they
  play out in everyday workplace interactions and how
  best to interrupt them.

- Chapter 5 points out that talking about "white male
  privilege" overlooks bias based on social class origin
  and age—and also that social forces aren't the sum
  total of people's life experiences. The kinds of measures that help first-gen white men will disproportionately help people of color, given that two-thirds
  of first-gen college students are people of color.[18]

- Chapters 6 and 7 discuss company cultures. Chapter 6
  provides a simple road map that shows how to pre-
  serve valued company cultures without sacrificing diversity. Chapter 7 addresses the fear that tackling DEI
  issues will require companies to become rigid and

bureaucratic. It describes a case study where a small shift toward more-structured performance evaluations had large positive effects.

- Chapters 8 and 9 discuss maternal wall bias, work–life conflict, and how the shift to remote work due to Covid-19 can help achieve DEI goals.

- Chapter 10 discusses whether businesses can just hire more women and people of color and be done with it, and explains how tug-of-war bias can doom that strategy.

- Chapters 11 and 12 are designed for CEOs. They provide a playbook for how your company can finally deliver on its DEI goals.

- Chapters 13 and 14 offer tools for chief diversity officers (CDOs) and heads of HR.

- Chapter 15 provides simple steps any manager can take to level the playing field—and ensure that everyone can do their best work.

Finally, throughout the book, I've indicated where we have additional worksheets or tool kits on our website, www .biasinterrupters.org. These are all free, based on established social science, and in some cases, have been shown through experiments in real companies to improve outcomes for people of color and white women. Some are designed to help HR professionals or organizational leaders; others, team leaders; and still others, employees. I think you'll have the best chance of achieving your DEI goals if you use those worksheets in concert with this book, so reminders about them will appear throughout the book. You can download them all in a printer-friendly format at www.biasinterrupters .org/book.

This book is organized around the questions and objections I commonly hear when people let their guard down and tell me what they actually think about diversity efforts. I used this structure for my last book, and found that readers love it because they can easily get answers to questions they have wondered about but don't feel comfortable asking. Also, reporters and producers love it because they know what questions to ask without reading the book carefully (or at all!).

CHAPTER 2

Is bias training worthless?

"Treat people as if they were what they should be, and you help them become what they are capable of."

—Johann Wolfgang von Goethe

Bias training has gotten a bad rap recently. This chapter will describe a new approach to bias training that provides the foundation for the new DEI playbook.

One bad-rap study, published in 2006, has been so influential that it's worth discussing in depth. Three sociologists—Alexandra Kalev, Frank Dobbin, and Erin Kelly—analyzed US Equal Employment Opportunity Commission data from more than 700 firms between 1971 and 2002, and examined whether certain common practices, including bias training, increased diversity. The study found that organizations that used diversity training increased representation of Black men by 4.5 percent—but white women's representation stayed flat and Black women's actually decreased nearly 6 percent.[1]

Their underlying point is well taken: companies should not rely on one-shot training sessions to solve DEI challenges.

But sometimes, in articles they wrote to disseminate their findings, their hostility to training goes a bit too far: "Hundreds of studies dating back to the 1930s suggest that anti-bias training doesn't reduce bias, alter behavior, or change the workplace."[2] First of all, in later analyses they found that voluntary manager training had significant positive effects, increasing representation of Black men, Latinos, and Asian American men and women. Moreover, two meta-analyses confirm that training can have positive effects on diversity knowledge and inclusion skills.[3] But there's a more basic point: all the trainings they assessed are now at least twenty years old. Early bias training tended to be sensitivity training. I agree that that kind of training was fated to fail. Businesses aim to solve business problems; increasing sensitivity and emotional expressiveness just ain't what most companies are designed to do.

Bottom line: Kalev, Dobbin, and Kelly found "garbage in, garbage out"[4]—bad trainings yield few good results.

Their study didn't address what is probably the dominant form of bias training today, which emerged circa 2000 and is based on the Implicit Association Test. The IAT provides an objective measure of bias by measuring *response latency*. That's a fancy name for an intuitive concept: associations that fit stereotypes happen milliseconds faster than those that don't. Most of us more quickly associate an oven mitt with women and a baseball mitt with men. The IAT measures those milliseconds.

Though IAT-based trainings were a definite improvement over the prior generation of sensitivity-based trainings, they have three main limitations. First, they focus on the wrong stage of the mental process. Research shows that it's extraordinarily difficult to avoid triggering stereotypes. Stereotype activation is automatic, but stereotype application can be controlled.[5] Second, research (discussed below) shows that changing behavior doesn't necessarily hinge on changing implicit biases. The third problem is even bigger: most IAT-based trainings focus on the cognitive bases of bias without much or any description of what bias at work really looks like, and with little or no guidance on how to interrupt it.

Luckily, there's an even newer generation of diversity trainings, and there's evidence that they work. A randomized controlled trial of a gender bias training given at the University of Wisconsin found that when at least 25 percent of a department attended the workshop, three months later faculty members were more likely to report taking actions to promote gender equity. Faculty in departments that got the workshop also reported feeling that they "fit" with their colleagues better, that colleagues valued their work more, and that they were more comfortable raising work-life conflicts.[6] A subsequent study found evidence of increased hiring of women, too.[7]

What was the bias training that produced these results? First, it introduced participants to the social science on bias. Then participants were asked to envision and write down how they would interrupt bias in the future. The focus was not on trying to suppress stereotypes, but instead on correcting for bias because we know it may well occur—a concept I call *cognitive override*. The workshop did not yield a significant decrease in implicit bias, but that didn't matter—further evidence that IAT-based training is on the wrong track.

My team developed a similar approach and has tried it with companies in a broad range of industries. Like the Wisconsin training, our message is: here's the evidence that bias exists and here's how it commonly plays out at work—and now that you know, how might you feel comfortable interrupting it? In our workshop, after presenting the social science, we provide a simple scenario of a particular kind of bias playing out and ask colleagues in groups of six to eight (in person or on Zoom) to talk through ideas for interrupting bias in that scenario. Like the Wisconsin training, this mobilizes a key insight: people are more likely to follow through if they precommit to taking a concrete step.[8] Our workshop goes one step further, reflecting research that found that training with more social interaction is more effective,[9] and that (not surprisingly!) people are more likely to take action when their colleagues respond positively to their efforts to use what they learned in diversity training.[10]

Both workshops also reflect the insights of self-determination theory, again a fancy name for a simple insight: people don't like to be bossed around, even by their bosses. Self-determination theory says we all have needs for competence, autonomy, and connection ("relatedness").[11] The new generation of trainings increase *competence* by explaining what bias looks like, and they give participants the *autonomy* to figure out bias interrupters that will work for them. Our workshop also supports *relatedness* by helping people connect with others at their workplace to set new norms and practices.

This approach can work in environments where sensitivity training doesn't. A dramatic example comes from when I was invited to give a workshop for department chairs at a major university. The folks who invited me were nervous because the chairs had been intensely negative about a diversity trainer a few years before. But I received no pushback whatsoever; in fact, 100 percent of those who filled out evaluations said they learned new ways of interrupting bias, and 83 percent said they would use them going forward. We get similar numbers again and again with many different types of organizations.

Mind you, these department chairs were mostly scientists, so they have a soft spot for data—but most professionals do. Our workshop introduces the five patterns of bias, explains how the lab studies provide objective evidence of bias, and shows how Workplace Experiences Survey data indicates that the same patterns of bias documented in those studies are reported at work.

But an important point: the goal is not to convince participants that they are biased even though they think they aren't—the key thrust of the Implicit Association Test. Instead, our focus is simply on stating (with data) that bias exists in the world and that they can play an active role in interrupting it. This helps defuse *identity threat*: people are highly motivated to defend themselves against threats that diminish their sense of competence, dignity, or self-worth.[12] If people think you're calling them bad, they will hunker down and circle the wagons. Approaching them with a good-faith assumption—that they are interested in helping redress problems that are corroding meritocracy for everyone—invites them to be their best selves.

When we give our workshop, we make sure that it describes examples that resonate—customized to the organization—so that it is tactical, not theoretical. This is easy to do, because if we describe the five patterns of bias to an experienced HR or diversity professional, typically they can give examples of how each pattern plays out at their company. Occasionally, we find that a pattern does not play out in a given workplace—which is great—but we introduce it anyway, say with an example of how it might happen with a client or supplier.

Increasingly, companies use the Workplace Experiences Survey so that the training can present their own data. The alternative is to present evidence from our national samples.[13] Either way, the training uses quotes and scenarios that describe what actually happens at the company. An important decision is whether the company wants to disclose that the quotes and scenarios included in the workshop come from within. Some prefer this, which means that if there is pushback, the trainer can respond, "I hate to say it, but this actually happened here." In companies that prefer not to do this, when workshop participants exclaim, "That's exactly what happens here," then the trainer says mildly, "Well, I guess I'm not surprised, because we find it's very pervasive."

Here's an example. After presenting the evidence of prove-it-again bias, we introduce the "stolen idea" problem: our research shows that while about one-third of men report that other people get credit for ideas they originally offered, close to half of all women (and two-thirds of multiracial women) architects do.[14]

After presenting this data, we ask: "You're in a meeting, and you just witnessed a stolen idea. How do you interrupt this bias?"

In the small group discussions, sometimes someone will ask, "Does that really happen here?" to which colleagues typically say, "Yup, it totally does." But then the discussion focuses not on whether it happens but on what to do when it does. Sometimes an eager beaver will announce that they'd say, "Hey, that's bias!" to which I respond, "If that works for you, fantastic. Does anyone have a different approach for someone who doesn't have the political capital to call it out?" People look at me with relief, as if to say, "OK, this person is not politically clueless; she recognizes that I'm just not going to spend all my chips calling out bias." Then they offer other ideas, and inevitably someone comes up with something: "I've been thinking about that idea, Tim, ever since Leticia first said it. You've added something important, maybe this is the next step." Sometimes more senior people say they would be far more direct: "Leticia, I think you originally suggested that—credit where credit is due." That can lead into an important conversation about the role leaders can play in setting social norms within the group.

Some people can afford to be very direct. When Google rolled out its bias training, its message was that Googlers should call out bias when they saw it. At a 2015 tech conference Judith Williams, at that time the head of Google's unconscious bias program, did just that—calling out Eric Schmidt, then the company's chair, for interrupting a woman on the panel with him several times.[15] God bless. One friend of mine, when someone stole her idea, looked him straight in the eye and asked, "Is there an echo here?" But she was the general counsel of the company. It's not realistic to expect people in less powerful positions to do this, and it's important to give people strategies they will actually use.

When our workshop is given in person, the dynamic in the room can be electric. Once I led it for a department of about two hundred people at a major tech company. I asked them to share strategies they came up with after discussing the stolen idea, and the first man to raise his hand said, "This is what I would do!" and gave some good advice.

The room broke into applause.

Research shows that in well-managed teams, the ratio of positive to negative feedback is in the range of 6:1.[16] Any bias trainer should keep this in mind. You have to give a whole lot of positive feedback to make space for the negative feedback that needs to be said.

Even though I'm a lawyer, our workshop never mentions the law. One of Dobbin and Kalev's important findings is that trainings should not mention legal liability but instead should focus on how diversity can enhance managers' ability to do their jobs.[17] This makes sense: people respond better to attempts to help them be successful than to threats of legal liability, which send them into a defensive "compliance crouch." (I discuss how to build the business case for diversity for your company in chapter 11.)

Another important message to convey in bias trainings is that leveling the playing field improves conditions for everyone. The Wisconsin experiment found that men and women reported improvements in organizational climate at about the same rates.[18] As will be discussed in chapter 7, we did an experiment that found that implementing measures to interrupt bias in performance evaluations increased constructive, concrete feedback for every group—including white men.

Another hotly contested topic is whether bias training should be mandatory. Kalev, Dobbin, and Kelly's research convinces me that garbage in/garbage out training should not be mandatory. But I don't think bias training should always be optional. How can people correct for gender bias if they don't know, for example, that gender bias fuels their instinct to fault women for what they see as admirable leadership behaviors in men? How can white people correct for racial bias if they don't know that requiring more evidence of competence from people of color reflects bias, not mere caution?

Kalev and Dobbin's opposition to mandatory training may in part reflect their experience as professors. Professors expect extremely high levels of autonomy, and hate to be bossed around—take it from me, that's one of the reasons we become professors. At many companies, however, managers are more used to having to get with the program, and more used to trainings on a wide variety of issues, from workplace safety to IT protocols.

There are definite costs to making bias training optional. Not surprisingly, research shows that when training is voluntary, those who need it least are most likely to show up. One study found that only about a quarter of people whose pretraining competence was lowest opted for training; close to three-quarters of those whose competence was highest did.[19]

All that said, there is a rare circumstance when I think bias workshops should be voluntary: where there's such a backlash against diversity that making them mandatory will result in a group of people sitting in the back and rolling their eyes. With the Workplace Experiences Survey, it's easy to find out whether your company has this level of backlash.

Does your company have a backlash against diversity? Use these survey items to find out. Ask people if they agree with the following statements:

- Focusing on diversity means lowering the bar for women and people of color.

- People are too focused on diversity at this organization.

- People should be more focused on quality and less focused on diversity at this organization.

In one company we worked with, nearly a third of white men thought that diversity measures were corroding meritocracy. We made attendance at the workshop optional but recommended that the CEO strongly signal that attendance was a good idea. That's something the CEO should do whether a workshop is mandatory or not.

Ultimately, whether bias training is mandatory is beside the point. To interrupt bias effectively, information about the five bias patterns should be fully integrated into the company's learning and development curriculum, as part of building bias interrupters into basic business systems. When hiring, you can't tap the full talent pool unless you control for bias, because you may well be holding women and people of color to higher standards. To write a fair performance evaluation, you have to know not to label women and people of color "difficult" for behavior that would be accepted without comment in a white man. To make compensation decisions, you have to correct for performance reward bias—white men tend to get higher raises than other groups with identical evaluations.[20] And on and on. So all of your company's programming—from onboarding to leadership training—should seamlessly build in continuing education on how bias enters company culture and how to interrupt it. Rather than being a once-a-year or once-in-a-lifetime thing, bias interruption should be included throughout the year—and year after year—at many evidence-based, meet-you-where-you're-at touchpoints.

Bias training should be part of an integrated approach

You can't bust bias with a workshop. You can interrupt it, but the minute you stop doing so, bias will pop back up like poisonous mushrooms.

The limitations of any bias workshop are built into the name of ours: it's called Individual Bias Interrupters because it provides strategies that any individual can use. But having individuals interrupt bias after it occurs is not enough. Unless you interrupt the constant transmission of bias throughout your workplace systems, as well as in day-to-day interactions, your company is making it difficult and time-consuming for people to interrupt bias even if they want to. A workshop just provides people the language and the background to understand why the company is tweaking business systems—to interrupt bias on an ongoing basis and at a structural level. To learn how to do that, read on.

CHAPTER 3

We're a meritocracy. Are you asking us to change that?

"Students' mental image of what their respected engineering professor should look like is a white balding male. I enter the classroom and I don't fit that image, so I start out with, 'OK, I have to prove myself to them.'"

—Latina professor

Black players need more experience than whites in order to get coaching jobs in the National Football League, and Black coaches get fewer second chances after a bad season.[1] It wasn't until symphony orchestra auditions were finally done "blind," despite the strong protestations of the offended music directors, that the percentage of women hired in top orchestras climbed from roughly 20 percent to 40 percent, even though over the same fifty-year period, 50 percent of Juilliard graduates were women.[2] Innumerable and independently validated data points suggest that our organizations are less meritocratic than we'd like to believe. For the success of DEI efforts, it's crucial to understand illusion and reality when it comes to meritocracy.[3]

Meritocracy is the unspoken backdrop to any DEI initiative

Most of us believe in meritocracy. Unless managers and employees can reconcile DEI goals with our preexisting commitment to meritocracy, many won't truly be on board with DEI goals, even if they say they are.

Meritocratic beliefs cluster around two related ideas: one, hard work pays off, and two, people generally get what they deserve based on their skill and effort.[4]

Americans in particular are so deeply committed to their belief in meritocracy that they even misremember nonmeritocratic explanations as meritocratic. In one experiment, subjects were asked to perform a task and told that Brooklyn College students would assess how well they did. When asked whether they thought the students were competent enough to make this assessment, subjects typically said they were, citing meritocratic reasons 33 percent of the time even when nothing was said about the students' competence or they'd been given a nonmeritocratic reason (e.g., that the Brooklyn students got the job because they had an "in" with the professor).[5] Americans' belief in meritocracy is so deep that many display psychological threat responses (agitation and anxiety) when that belief is challenged.[6]

Sadly, meritocracy doesn't exist as much as we hope, wish, and believe it does. It's not meritocracy when some groups have to prove themselves more than others—like Black players who need more experience than whites to get coaching jobs—and when mistakes are more costly for some groups than others, like the Black coaches who are given fewer second chances than whites after a bad season.[7] Nor is it meritocracy when a woman musician can't get a job unless a music director doesn't know she's a woman.

Investing time to understand the research here is critically important because fears that DEI efforts will undermine meritocracy are very real: a third of the white men in one company we worked with thought DEI was corroding it.[*] They said things like this:

> Merit is vastly more important than gender or race, and efforts to "balance" gender and race diminish the overall quality of an organization by reducing the collective merit of the personnel.

> I have never witnessed sexism, racism, or any other diversity issues at [company name]. I do think the company is becoming way too political, and is wasting too much time on this issue.

---

[*]Where no source is given, the information is from one of the companies we have worked with. We have worked with many companies, so no one should jump to conclusions about the firm's identity.

Backlash against DEI is particularly strong in engineering because of the sense that the field is pure and inherently "rigorous" and that importing extraneous "political" considerations will corrode quality.[8] But worries about meritocracy are not limited to engineering. And—sad but true—research shows that organizations that see themselves as meritocratic actually show more bias than those that don't.[9]

There's no easy answer to overcoming the belief that "we are already a meritocracy," but one thing's for sure: in most organizations, talking about evidence will work better than talking about empathy.

Prove-it-again bias has been documented for decades

We need to start with the evidence, and there's plenty of it. In this and subsequent chapters, I summarize forty years of social science, documenting bias by race, gender, class, and age. Our extensive bibliography (at www.biasinterrupters .org) includes studies from experimental social psychology, industrial-organizational psychology, sociology, and behavioral economics.[10]

Over and over, these studies find that meritocracy is corroded because some groups have to prove themselves more than others. Here are a few questions that uncover prove-it-again bias, which stems from "lack of fit."[11]

Imagine a brilliant tech founder. Or an up-and-coming investment banker. Or a hard-driving litigator. Or an engineer.

Does your company have prove-it-again bias? Use these survey items to find out. Ask people if they agree with the following statements:

- I have to prove myself over and over again to get the same level of recognition as my colleagues.

- When I give outstanding performance, people seem surprised.

- People tend to dismiss it as luck when I perform well at work.

If you're like most people, a white man came to mind. Because other groups don't seem as good a fit, they need to provide more evidence of competence than white men do. A dramatic example was when the late renowned Stanford neuroscientist Ben Barres gave a talk and heard that a colleague commented, "Ben Barres gave a great seminar today, but then his work is so much better than his sister's."[12]

It was the same work: Ben was a transgender man who began his career as Barbara Barres. But Ben fit the image of a neuroscientist, so the work was seen as better when it came from Ben than when it came from Barbara.

White men are seen as a better fit for virtually all high-level jobs in virtually every well-paid field; that's why more-rigorous standards are applied to women and people of color reaching for those jobs.[13] Women scientists of color are eloquent on the topic. *"The vision of the scientist is the white guy with the glasses,"* said a Latina in biomedical research. *"If you don't fit the stereotype, you are not going to be taken seriously."* How does this play out? A Latina science professor was regularly mistaken for a janitor even when wearing her lab coat. As she put it, *"I always amuse my friends with my janitor stories."* She calmly informed people she only had keys to her office, not the custodian's closet.[14]

Our data shows that women of color are at least four times more likely than white men to report having been mistaken for admins, janitorial staff, court reporters, etc., with Black women most affected (see figure 3-1).

FIGURE 3-1

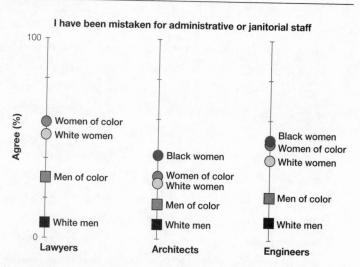

I have been mistaken for administrative or janitorial staff

Note: "Women of color" and "Men of color" include all people who identified as Black, Asian or Asian American, Latinx or Hispanic, multiracial, or any other nonwhite option. The data for the "of color" group provides an average of the data for each specific group.

Where available, the graphs highlight the group whose experiences diverge the most from white men's. When a single group is not highlighted, the percentage differentials between the individual groups were too small to be meaningful.

Our research shows prove-it-again bias plays out in both industrywide and company samples. Typically, one-quarter to one-third of white men, but roughly half to three-quarters of women and people of color, report having to prove themselves more than their colleagues, with Black women most affected. Among architects, women and people of color are approximately twice as likely as white men to report having to prove themselves more than their colleagues do (see figure 3-2).[15]

Women of color report the highest rates of prove-it-again bias because they face negative competence assumptions

FIGURE 3-2

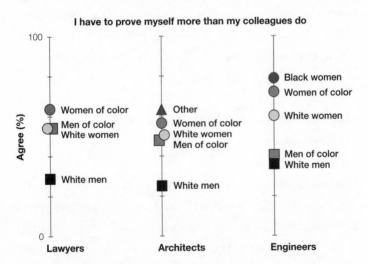

I have to prove myself more than my colleagues do

Note: "Women of color" and "Men of color" include all people who identified as Black, Asian or Asian American, Latinx or Hispanic, multiracial, or any other nonwhite option. The data for the "of color" group provides an average of the data for each specific group. "Other" includes other underrepresented people.

Where available, the graphs highlight the group whose experiences diverge the most from white men's. When a single group is not highlighted, the percentage differentials between the individual groups were too small to be meaningful.

based on both race and gender. This pattern carries over in industry after industry, and workplace after workplace. In fourteen studies totaling 17,824 people in many different fields, we repeatedly find that women and people of color reported having to prove themselves more than white men by large percentages. Remember: even small differences add up quickly over time.[16] Again, our studies with self-reported data is supported by a broad array of experimental studies.

Among women of color, Black women often report the highest levels of prove-it-again bias. Over three-quarters of Black women scientists, as compared with roughly two-thirds of every other group of women, report having to prove themselves more than colleagues of similar education and experience. If you eliminate prove-it-again bias for Black women, you can eliminate it for everyone else.

Prove-it-again bias results from a series of cognitive biases

Prove-it-again bias occurs at the level of cognitive processing, creating double standards documented by social psychologist Monica Biernat and many others.[17] Indeed, at the core of most stereotypes of women and people of color, especially in work contexts, is the idea that they are less competent.[18] Here are three major ways this plays out at work:

Mistakes matter more

In a meritocracy, everyone's mistakes are equally costly, or equally easily forgiven. That's not what happens in reality. Mistakes of groups that "don't fit" are more likely to be noticed and remembered.[19] One experiment sent memos with a number of mistakes to law firm partners, who noticed twice as many mistakes in memos with Black-sounding names as in identical memos with white-sounding names.[20] Mistakes also are more costly: white males' mistakes led to firing and/or formal reports of incompetence less often than when identical mistakes were believed to come from women or Black men.[21]

Our interview evidence shows the end result. *"White associates are not expected to be perfect. Black associates . . . have one chance, and if you mess up that chance, look out,"* said a Black lawyer. And it's not just law. *"I have seen white males who make extremely costly mistakes on projects—where the firm or insurance had to pay for it—get a slap on the wrist or even be promoted, while I have seen women who made one bad decision be forced out,"* said an Asian American architect.[22] A woman in a large company commented, *"For women, you make one mistake . . . and you are out, thrown to the side, no longer considered for opportunity. For men, they can make many mistakes. The other men cover for them."*

Successes matter less

A classic 1974 experiment found that women's success on male-typed tasks tends to be attributed to outside causes like luck; men's is attributed to internal qualities like skill.[23]

Basically, every high-level professional job is seen as a male task. Memory is driven by stereotypes too: in one experiment, subjects were asked to recall an Asian American woman college applicant's math SAT score. When asked about "the female high school student," they recalled lower scores than when asked about "the Asian high school student," reflecting stereotypes that Asians are good at math and women aren't.[24] In another study, across three experiments, subjects rated a female team member as less competent and influential than a male team member who had acted in precisely the same way.[25] In architecture, only 8 percent of white men, but nearly two to three times that percentage of every other group, reported accomplishments discounted as luck.[26]

All this adds up: if your successes are overlooked, forgotten, or written off as "just luck," you need more successes to succeed.

Benefit of the doubt isn't equally distributed. In a meritocracy, either everyone gets the benefit of the doubt or no one does. But research shows that in-groups typically get it, while out-groups don't.[27] *"Women are promoted when there is no other option other than to promote them, in their late fifties. Men are promoted in their late thirties to the same roles, even if it is a stretch,"* said a Latina architect. *"Coldly objective judgment seems to be reserved for members of out-groups,"* psychologist Marilynn Brewer notes wryly.[28] In the late 1990s, Brewer explored the ways in which discrimination stems not just from dislike of out-groups but also from preferential treatment of in-groups, notably through *leniency bias*—when objective rules are applied rigorously to out-groups and leniently to in-groups. The study of in-group favoritism dates back to 1954.[29]

Contemporary studies show how this plays out at work. A 2020 study of tech workers by Shelley Correll and her colleagues found that women who received feedback that they needed to acquire new skills to get to the next level received lower ratings than men who received similar feedback.[30] Note the confidence that men will grow, accompanied by worries that women won't.

Interviews show that men are judged on potential but women need demonstrated competence. *"I have to prove myself to . . . colleagues before I can get the respect that a male will get by default,"* said a professor. Said a woman lawyer, *"They were saying, 'We don't know her book of business,' yet they let the males slide through . . . The scrutiny of a woman's book of business is harder."*

Halo vs. horns

First documented around 1920, this pattern describes when one piece of evidence leads to an overall assessment.[31] Those who fit often get "halos" (one strength is generalized into an overall positive assessment), while those who don't get "horns" (one weakness is generalized into a negative one). Horns explain why mistakes matter more for women and people of color: one mistake leads to a negative assessment. Halos explain why white men are judged on potential without the need for demonstrated competence: one success leads to confidence in their potential for future successes.

Prove-it-again bias corrodes meritocracy

Prove-it-again bias starts at hiring but does not end there since, as we know, women and people of color may find themselves assumed incompetent once in the job. *"I reiterated the information we needed . . . He could not answer me, so I asked again in another way. He told me that I wouldn't understand the answer because it's too complicated for me. I explained I'd done the job for two years, so I understood. He then told me to 'calm down' and started talking down to me even more,"* said a white woman engineer. *"I had clients refer all their questions to my twenty-something male intern, when I was a forty-something owner of the company,"* explained an Asian American architect. And women are less likely than men to get credit for work done in a team—of course, most work is done in teams.[32]

The end result: *"Women have to look more professional and demonstrate technical prowess at all times to receive the same respect as a male engineer who is just an average engineer,"* said one woman.

The size of the prove-it-again effect is easiest to measure in the field of science.[33] According to one study, women postdocs need to be twice as productive to receive the same competency rating as men, and women scientists need the equivalent of three more papers in *Nature* or *Science* or twenty more—twenty!—in less prestigious journals.[34]

That's not meritocracy.

Prove-it-again bias is triggered by many social categories, including race, gender, class origin, sexual orientation, age, and disability; in all cases, lower-status groups are seen as less competent than higher-status groups.[35] Again, this is old news: an influential early study was published in 1972.[36]

Women of color, who face two sets of negative competence assumptions—race and gender—consistently report the highest levels of prove-it-again bias in our surveys.[37] The divergence between the experiences of white men and Black women can be particularly dramatic.[38] The end result: *"There's just no room for error. To the extent that other folks might feel that they can have a bad day . . . I never feel I have that luxury. You're just always on, and if you're not on, you'd better make people think you're on,"* said a Black lawyer for a major company.[39]

Prove-it-again bias affects success at every job stage

Maybe we should call it prove-it-again-and-again-and-again bias. Because it never really goes away, even when someone has established a track record of excellence. Consider four common workplace contexts:

Hiring

Countless matched-résumé studies document bias in hiring.[40] One of the most elegant was a 2012 randomized controlled trial (RCT) that found that identical résumés of a man and a woman resulted in the man being judged more competent, more likely to be hired and mentored, and deserving of a higher salary. RCTs are the gold standard of research and track precisely what we found in our data on self-reported bias.[41]

If your company isn't keeping track of when objective job requirements are waived, it should be. Because of leniency bias, objective requirements often are applied rigorously to out-groups but leniently to in-groups. As one white woman recalled, *"We rejected a lot of . . . candidates because they had not worked at a [company like ours] but then hired a man who hadn't either. He knew someone, so they let him in the pool."*

Meritocracy can also be undermined when whatever qualification men happen to have is more valued. One study involved hiring for a police job that required both education and experience. When the male candidate had more education but less experience than the female candidate, people tended to choose the man, explaining that it was because he had more education. But when he had more experience and less education than she did, people again chose him, this time saying it was because he had more experience.[42] Whichever qualification the man had more of was deemed more essential to the job. Heads I win, tails you lose.

Beware also of hiring or promotion criteria that effectively block one group. To illustrate the point, does your job really need someone who has been a fighter pilot—or does it need only someone who has the disposition of a fighter pilot? Does your job require that someone has held a similar role in a similar company—or just have demonstrated certain skills under pressure? Defining requirements in terms of work skills and dispositions nearly always makes more sense, but it is particularly important not to require experiences that largely exclude women or people of color if your goal is to recruit and promote them.

One key to controlling prove-it-again bias in hiring is to create a preagreed structure and follow a disciplined process for evaluating résumés and structuring interviews. In ranking résumés and interview performance, use a rubric and apply it consistently. Prove-it-again bias thrives when you rely on gut-level decision making or fly by the seat of your pants.

Promotions

Leniency bias affects promotion in many ways.[43] *"For a woman to get a promotion—it's difficult. I've actually been doing the job, without the title or a pay raise, for about a year. But they still needed more time to see whether I was up to it,"* said a woman in tech, an industry where we hear of this pattern again and again. Companies should be keeping track of whether it takes longer for women or people of color to get promoted, and if so, take active steps to control for bias as a key suspect.

Sometimes people report that good performance is discounted even after they have met all the requirements for promotion. To quote a Latina professor, *"When I went up for promotion, [questions were asked about] whether or not I would continue to be doing the things I was doing once I got full professor. I had never heard that kind of comment ever expressed in [men's] deliberations. It was a double standard."*

Prove-it-again bias can lead to "underleveling" (placing someone at a lower level than their skills would justify).

"A woman can manage 35 percent more staff than a man but still be rated as underperforming," said a woman in a large company. In this company, less than one-fifth of white men, but about two-thirds of Black employees, reported that they had seen someone of their race or gender underleveled.

The best way to spot prove-it-again bias in promotions is to keep track of whom you promote. If only one group gets ahead, you need to ask some searching questions and consider whether there is bias in the system.

Performance evaluations

Because performance evaluations leave a written record, they've been a gold mine for researchers studying bias—including my team. In our study of a Wall Street law firm, we found women's successes discounted: women got more positive comments than men on their performance evaluations, but men got higher ratings—men's positive comments predicted high rankings, but women's did not.[44] A 2020 study of tech found the same thing: women with the same feedback got lower evaluations.[45]

When men are judged on potential but women on performance, this affects performance evaluations: "For a male associate, [the evaluations] would read, 'They haven't had the opportunity to get real trial experience, but we have all the confidence in the world that he has all the capability to be a success,'" said a woman general counsel. "Then, for a female associate, and I am talking about some of the most exceptional young attorneys, they would say, 'She has not had the opportunity to get any real trial experience, and so the jury is still out.'"[46] In tech, because men "look the part," they more often received comments that they were "visionary," and such comments raised men's ratings more than women's, found the 2020 study.[47] This is hard to overcome—the stage seems already set.

It also affects performance evaluations when some groups' mistakes matter more.[48] When we audited one company's evaluations, 43 percent of people of color had a mistake mentioned; only 28 percent of white people did.

Any process, including performance evaluations, that requires informal horse-trading unmoored from data is a petri dish for bias. Calibration meetings where candidates are rank-ordered allow bias to run rampant unless they're conducted with evidence, consistent grading rubrics to be certain everyone is assessed on the same things, and care to ensure that harsher standards are not applied to particular groups. To help with this, start by tracking data about the rankings assigned by the graders, and then separately track rankings assigned after data is debated—and decide in advance what the weight of specific factors should be. Often, in calibration meetings, Candidate 1's higher scores on X will be used to justify a higher overall ranking while ignoring his low score on Y; Candidate 2's higher scores on Z will be used to justify a high ranking while ignoring his poor performance on X; Candidate 3 will have all her scores counted and be rewarded only if she lacks any weakness. This is precisely where prove-it-again bias creeps in.

Meetings

Men are often expected to have brilliant ideas because they "look the part."[49] So what happens when a woman has one? There's a good chance it's misremembered as coming from a man. Among lawyers, about half of women, but only a third of men, report that other people get credit for ideas they originally offered, which reflects confirmation bias: we see what we expect to see.[50] A white woman architect told us, *"We have a firm-wide women's initiative . . . and they said that one of the number-one complaints from women architects was that they would bring up something in a design meeting; it would be ignored. Then a man would say it, and then people would recognize it."* This happens so often that it became a popular FedEx commercial, where a manager repeated exactly what someone else had just said, waving his hand for emphasis; he got all the credit, with everyone in the room clapping. The person with the original idea complains to a colleague, who responds: "Yeah but you didn't do this," repeating the manager's signature hand wave.

This happens to people of color of all genders: "I've been in meetings where we'd go around the table. I offer an idea. Nobody acknowledges it. A couple of seconds later, a white guy at the table offers the exact same idea, and everybody thinks it's brilliant. [It's] . . . happened to me many times," said Greg Moore, chair of a mentoring program for a well-known Black fraternity.[51] While about a third of white men in architecture report that other people get credit for ideas they originally offered, close to half of white women do. Multiracial women reported losing credit for their ideas at

FIGURE 3-3

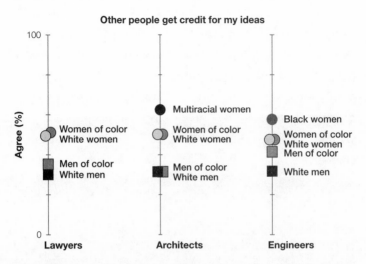

Other people get credit for my ideas

Note: "Women of color" and "Men of color" include all people who identified as Black, Asian or Asian American, Latinx or Hispanic, multiracial, or any other nonwhite option. The data for the "of color" group provides an average of the data for each specific group.

Where available, the graphs highlight the group whose experiences diverge the most from white men's. When a single group is not highlighted, the percentage differentials between the individual groups were too small to be meaningful.

an even higher rate (see figure 3-3). Other industries show similar patterns.

If other people get credit for your ideas, you need to have a lot more of them to get ahead.

Interrupt prove-it-again bias

To create a true meritocracy, organizations need to interrupt prove-it-again bias. Three generalizable principles exist for doing so. The first is to ensure decisions take the same criteria into account for everyone, which requires making those criteria explicit. The second is to require evidence to show the criteria have been met; people should have to prove it, rather than just saying it. The third key is accountability: people who have to explain their decisions exhibit less bias than people who don't.[52] The bottom line is structure and discipline. Doing things on the fly, without evidence and without standards, is rocket fuel for bias. More about this in chapter 7.

CHAPTER 4

Why do some groups need to be politically savvier to succeed?

"I have learned that . . . as a woman, I can't get away with as much as a man."

—White woman

Black NFL players' victory dances result in higher yardage penalties and lower pay than white players' dances do.[1] This is emblematic of the fact that some groups can get away with more—sometimes a lot more—than others. *"I have found that it is much more accepted for a male to be aggressive. Many professors will even kick the doors and everything, and nobody seems to care about that. I can guarantee if a female does it, they will feel that she's crazy,"* said a Latina engineer. Sometimes it doesn't need to escalate to door-kicking to raise eyebrows: *"I strongly believe that my assertiveness in getting the job done would not be viewed negatively if I was male,"* said one white woman engineer.

This is just one way office politics are complicated for women and people of color. Finding the "right" way to respond to workplace racism is not something white people need to do, and finding the right way to respond to sexism is not something men need to do. *"At work, my boss accused me of being 'oversensitive,' of making things about race that aren't,"* said an Asian American lawyer.[2]

Handling racism the right way is important because it is common in the office. In our research, half of architects of color, and about two-thirds of Black ones, report racism at work.* A rigorous 2017 meta-analysis found, shockingly, no decrease in racial discrimination against Black Americans since 1989.[3] A 2020 study found that 30 percent of Asians and Asian Americans surveyed reported an increase in discrimination during the pandemic, including at work: *"I have heard the virus referred to by people I work with as the 'Chinese virus,'"* said one Asian American.[4]

Racism complicates the mini-politics of everyday work life

Racism can manifest in overt and even extreme ways, like a noose being left at the workstation of a Black person—which happened to an airplane mechanic in 2014—but in profes-

---

*Because our study of architects looked at racial bias in the most depth, the statistics and quotations in this section are from architects unless otherwise noted. We expect our findings in architecture to be generalizable to other white-collar professions, given that data from architecture parallels data from law and engineering on virtually all other questions in the Workplace Experiences Survey, although the differentials between white men and other groups vary in size.

sional environments typically it's more subtle.[5] *"Most of the racism is not overt, such as using derogatory terms or names, but is more subtle,"* said a man of color at a large company. *"Colleagues and managers are dismissive—not responding to calls or emails, or suggesting one is being overly sensitive. They are demeaning through daily microaggressions—not remembering your name, what you said in the meeting, or interrupting and not allowing you to speak in a meeting."* In our research, half of people of color and two-thirds of African Americans report having to deal with racism at work.

When I began to research race about a decade ago, I was struck by how commonly Black professionals described their interactions as "demeaning" or "disrespectful." *"I have experienced behavior that is unbecoming, like being patted on my head by my CEO . . . It was in a public place, and I was just mortified."* I continue to be struck by the tone of bleak isolation I hear from Black women. A Black woman biologist explained that she avoided socializing with her colleagues because *"if it's too social, I think there is a great risk of you being put in that subservient position and being looked at that way."*[6] This is what Pulitzer Prize–winning reporter Isabel Wilkerson means when she describes "America's caste system."[7] Sometimes it's perpetuated by "jokes." A multiracial woman recalled chatting with a Black coworker: *"She and I were the only nonwhite employees in the office . . . One of the firm's principals walked up to us and said, 'Stop distracting the help.'"*

Racial stereotypes are rampant. Half of Black architects report having to deal with them. Two-thirds of Black women, as compared with only a quarter of white men, report having to work extra hard to be seen as a team player; Black men fell in between (43 percent). African Americans are more likely than any other group to say they encounter racism and racial stereotypes, including others' belief that they have received unfair advantages—a contemporary trope on the theme that out-groups' successes get discounted or ignored. Figure 4-1 reports the largest effects.

Asian Americans are stereotyped as intelligent, hardworking, mathematical, self-disciplined . . . but also cunning, sly, selfish, nerdy, and lacking interpersonal warmth and kindness.[8] Astonishingly, Asian American women scientists report more prove-it-again bias than white women;

FIGURE 4-1

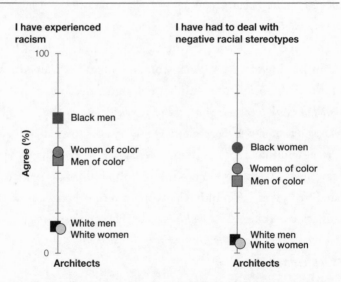

Note: "Women of color" and "Men of color" include all people who identified as Black, Asian or Asian American, Latinx or Hispanic, multiracial, or any other nonwhite option. The data for the "of color" group provides an average of the data for each specific group.

Where available, the graphs highlight the group whose experiences diverge the most from white men's.

the stereotype that Asian Americans are good at science doesn't help them.[9] About a third of Asian American architects report having to deal with negative racial stereotypes; roughly three in five report being seen as team players rather than leaders. Figure 4-2 reports the largest effects.

Asian Americans of both sexes are often seen as having technical skills but not potential to lead. *"As an Asian American man, I often felt firm leadership would overlook my leadership contributions and capabilities."* Asian American women

FIGURE 4-2

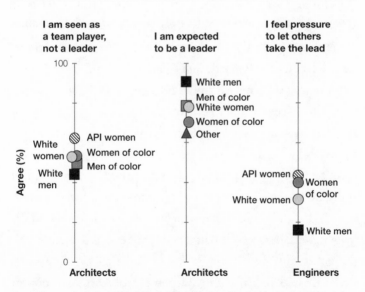

Note: "Women of color" and "Men of color" include all people who identified as Black, Asian or Asian American (API), Latinx or Hispanic, multiracial, or any other nonwhite option. The data for the "of color" group provides an average of the data for each specific group. We did not receive enough responses from male engineers of color to draw conclusions.

Where available, the graphs highlight the group whose experiences diverge the most from white men's.

encounter a different stereotype: "I've had opposing counsel treat me like a little girl, and part of that is the Asian thing because they see a little Asian doll . . . It's really annoying and I'm really tired of it,"[10] said a lawyer. Among architects, Asian American men are nearly three times as likely as white men to report they're expected to play a passive role. In engineering, 43 percent of Asian American women, but only 16 percent of white men, report pressure to let others take the lead. And sometimes Asian Americans are expected to do more work with fewer resources and less support because they're "such hard workers."[11] The "forever foreign" stereotype is particularly irritating: *"'How do Chinese feel about that?' Well, I don't really know. I grew up in a suburb in New Jersey,"* said an architect. *"I [grew up in Pittsburgh and] went to Princeton and Cornell. I should speak English 'surprisingly well,'"* mused a physicist. Some 33 percent of men of Asian descent and 44 percent of women of Asian descent say they've been asked "Where are you really from?" (see figure 4-3). And over one-third of architects of Asian descent reported that colleagues were surprised by their English skills, although many were born in the United States.

A 2016 study found that over two-thirds of Latinx adults in a nationally representative sample reported having experienced discrimination.[12] In our research on architects, nearly half of Latinas and 29 percent of Latinos reported having to deal with negative stereotypes. Half of Latinas and over one-third of Latinos reported being seen for their technical skills, not their leadership potential. Latinas also

FIGURE 4-3

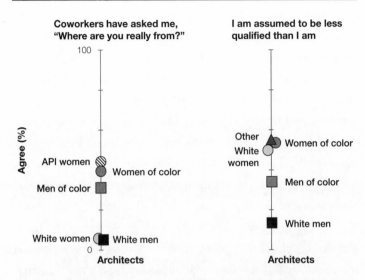

Note: "Women of color" and "Men of color" include all people who identified as Black, Asian or Asian American (API), Latinx or Hispanic, multiracial, or any other nonwhite option. The data for the "of color" group provides an average of the data for each specific group. "Other" includes other underrepresented people.

Where available, the graphs highlight the group whose experiences diverge the most from white men's.

were particularly likely to have been called "loud" when speaking in a normal tone of voice. Our research on scientists found that Latinas were more likely than any other group of women to say they did not feel free to express even justifiable anger at work.[13]

Latina scientists, too, reported startling forms of disrespect: one had a white male colleague who *"went so far as knocking on my head and saying, 'Is there anyone there?'"* Years later, recounting this story, her hands were shaking. She said it took her years to regain her confidence.

Other Latinx professionals pinpointed racist stereotypes that drive prove-it-again problems: *"There seems to be this stereotype that, if you are from Mexico, you are lazy and you only like to either sleep by a cactus or party."* Nearly half of Latinas, and nearly a third of Latinos, reported colleagues being surprised by their command of English, although many had been born in the United States. Again, there are the "jokes," as when a colleague said during a professional disagreement with a Latina, *"Oh, be careful, she's Puerto Rican, and she may be carrying a knife in her purse."*[14] Or, *"I was 'jokingly' asked to empty out my pockets when a coworker misplaced his tool, which turned out to be on his desk."* Latinas in tech who behave assertively risk getting called "feisty" or "sassy," our research shows.[15] These words are telling: both communicate that a low-status person does not know her place.

Navigating these stereotypes is intricate, draining, and sometimes depressing. A story explains the dilemmas. A male African American editor for a national newspaper was taken aback in a meeting when a young white man, more junior than he and with less experience—and who had come late to the meeting—described himself as *"responsible not just for what he did, but also for what I did and others did, as if he had oversight,"* which he did not. The editor said nothing for fear of coming off as an "aggressive Black man" and noted that his manager said nothing either.

When being "reasonable" means being deferential

The higher yardage penalties for Black NFL players is emblematic of complex politics in a second way. To succeed, white men typically need to be assertive and ambitious, but for other groups being deferential often is the price of being seen as reasonable. An experiment by sociologists Cecilia Ridgeway and Sandra Nakagawa found an "overwhelming pattern": that low-status members of a group who behaved deferentially were seen as reasonable and viewed with respect; they "knew their place."[16] This helps explain why people of color of all genders and women of all races face challenges when they behave authoritatively. It is also why women are less likely to take credit unless their contribution is crystal clear.[17]

What happens to people who don't know their place? Many, many studies since the 1970s by social psychologists, notably Laurie Rudman, Victoria Brescoll, Madeline Heilman, and Alice Eagly, document the "backlash against agentic women": women who display assertiveness, leadership, anger, self-promotion, or other forms dominance tend to trigger dislike.[18] Women who succeed in typically male jobs also tend to be disliked—and people who are disliked are seen as less competent than those who aren't. In other words, tightrope bias exacerbates prove-it-again bias.

Qualitative data confirms that women walk a tightrope between being seen as abrasive if they're assertive and unqualified if they aren't. *"To get ahead here,"* said an MIT professor, *"you have to be so aggressive. But women who are too aggressive are ostracized . . . and if they're not aggressive enough they have to do twice the work."* Navigating the likability/competence trade-off can be complicated and draining. *"It's exhausting to fight gender roles and play the balancing act of being assertive but not bitchy, helpful but not a doormat. It is exhausting on the good days, soul-crushing on the bad days,"* said a woman engineer.

The "good" woman is nurturing, expressive, and responsive to the needs of others—a good team player. Men are expected to be competitive, ambitious, direct, and assertive—leaders.[19] These stereotypes have actually *strengthened* in recent decades.[20]

The tightrope may be narrowest for Asian American women: in our study of scientists, nearly two-thirds report pushback for assertiveness, compared to roughly half of other groups of women.[21] Scientists of Asian descent also are far more likely than other women to report pressures to behave in feminine ways and pushback for self-promotion.[22] But it probably varies by industry. Among architects, Latinas, multiracial women, and other underrepresented people report the highest levels.[23]

This is why women who try to follow the male model of success—by being competitive and ambitious—often face backlash. *"Men are tough. Women are bitches."* An Asian American astrophysicist elaborated: *"If you're a young man, you're a boy genius. But if you're a young woman, you are so threatening that, in order . . . not to be intensely disliked by everybody else, I have had to be as amiable as possible and a group player all the time, not looking out for myself, so I damp down my ambition . . . I rarely talk about the prizes*

I get, the media attention I get." Note the no-win situation: hide your light under a bushel and never get ahead, or trumpet your accomplishments and never get ahead.

Savvy women make the necessary adjustments. *"Here's how men negotiate: 'No fucking way. That's never going to happen.' Here's how I have to negotiate: 'I hear what you're saying. I'm sympathetic. If I were in your shoes I would want that too.'"* This Wall Street lawyer was using "gender judo": doing a masculine thing in a feminine way in an attempt to dodge the backlash against assertive women.[24] Trying to figure out how to establish one's authority without triggering backlash is a lot more complicated than just having to act authoritatively. Politically astute women can figure it out—but that just means that political savvy is mandatory for women but optional for men. A study of female MBAs found that the most successful women displayed masculine traits with "high self-monitoring"—attention to how they were being perceived.[25]

Tightrope bias also shapes meeting dynamics. In meetings that include more men than women, women typically participate about 25 percent less than men.[26] Why? It's probably self-editing in the face of the stereotype so plainly voiced by the former head of the Tokyo 2020 Olympic committee, who resigned after complaining that women talk too much in meetings.[27] I'm not kidding: one response by Japan's ruling party was to invite women to an all-male meeting on the condition that they do not talk![28]

Men also interrupt women much more than vice versa. *"I have been interrupted and talked over in presentations with male partners at the firm, only to have my ideas and drawings credited to a young male staff person,"* said a woman architect. Men do this because it's seen as socially appropriate: he's competitive and ambitious, a man to be reckoned with. If women do the same thing, the response is "Who does she think she is?" Our research shows that white women in architecture and engineering are roughly three to five times more likely than white men to report being interrupted more than their colleagues in meetings. Other research shows that women are not only less likely to interrupt; they are also less likely to gain the floor when they do interrupt and are offered fewer chances to participate.[29] A study of economics seminars also found that women are challenged more than men and more likely to be asked hostile questions.[30]

Other studies confirm that race triggers tightrope bias too—notably those by Ashleigh Shelby Rosette, Erika Hall, and Robert Livingston.[31] They document that Black people often encounter backlash not only when doing celebration dances on the football field, but also when leading in work settings. Experiments by Jennifer Berdahl and Ji-A Min found that white Americans tend to dislike Asian Americans who behave in dominant ways.[32] Again, this data provides an objective measure that bias exists, controlling for all other factors. Other experiments show that the same behavior by different groups is judged very differently: one found that a female leader who expressed anger was judged as being "out of control" but a male leader who did the same was not. This was used to justify giving the female leader less pay, power, and status.[33] "He's having a bad day; she's emotional."[34]

Women and people of color may be seen as angry or emotional if they behave in ways that, in a white man, would likely be seen as showing career-enhancing passion for the business. *"When I advocated strongly for my position, people said I was getting 'too emotional,'"* said a white woman. *"I'm calm. I don't raise my voice . . . because if I were as assertive as some of my Caucasian colleagues that are male, I would be called a mad Black woman,"* said a microbiologist. *"I'm very candid and I do not hesitate to open my mouth and was probably not the submissive female person, [and now I have] a reputation of being a dragon lady,"* said another biologist. In a study, displays of anger during group deliberations increased men's influence but decreased women's—and though the study focused on gender rather than race, one suspects that this applies chiefly to white men.[35]

Sometimes women and people of color are invited into professional workplaces but expected to play a "worker bee" role, cheerfully grinding away without asking for recognition or advancement, with Black women the most affected.[36] Women and people of color are significantly more likely to report the expectation that they be worker bees. The largest divergence we found is between white men (34 percent) and Black women (64 percent) in architecture (see figure 4-4). Often this is accompanied by an expectation that certain groups should be grateful just to be there, and that expecting anything more is unreasonable.

Among architects, nearly two-thirds of Black women and 43 percent of Black men reported having to work harder than their colleagues to be seen as a team player. *"We are perceived as 'the help,' not the leaders, when oftentimes we are more capable of leading the job. Minorities having more degrees, more years of experience, more [qualifications] never equates to white*

FIGURE 4-4

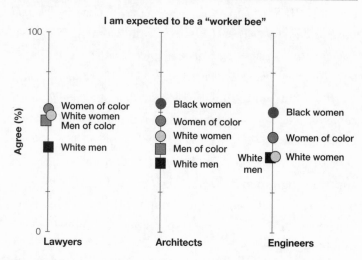

Note: "Women of color" and "Men of color" include all people who identified as Black, Asian or Asian American, Latinx or Hispanic, multiracial, or any other nonwhite option. The data for the "of color" group provides an average of the data for each specific group.

Where available, the graphs highlight the group whose experiences diverge the most from white men's. When a single group is not highlighted, the percentage differentials between the individual groups were too small to be meaningful.

males with less experience, as they are better-connected individuals. Constant country club behavior," said a multiracial architect.

Our research suggests that tightrope bias is stronger in some industries than others, and is more consistent and pronounced for women of all races than for men of color, with Asian American and Black women often affected the most. In law and engineering, nearly two-thirds of men report they seldom receive pushback for behaving assertively, as compared to about half of women. White men across industries overwhelmingly (85 percent to 90 percent) report they are seen as leaders; lower proportions of women and people of color say the same (see figure 4-5).

FIGURE 4-5

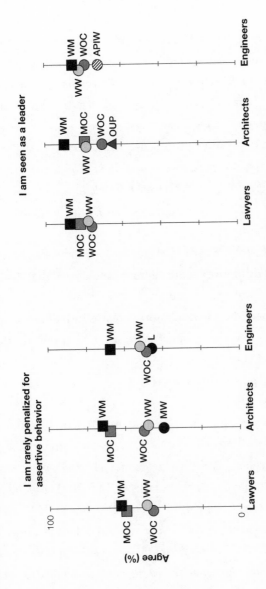

Note: WM = white men; WW = white women; MOC = men of color; WOC = women of color; L = Latinas; APIW = Asian/Pacific Islander women; MW = multiracial women; OUP = other underrepresented people.

"Women of color" and "Men of color" include all people who identified as Black, Asian or Asian American, Latinx or Hispanic, multiracial, or any other nonwhite option. The data for the "of color" group provides an average of the data for each specific group. We did not receive enough responses from male engineers of color to draw conclusions.

Where available, the graphs highlight the group whose experiences diverge the most from white men's. When a single group is not highlighted, the percentage differentials between the individual groups were too small to be meaningful.

How tightrope bias constricts access to opportunities

Tightrope bias has a dramatic impact on access to opportunities. *"I am a senior practitioner who has outstanding credentials but has routinely been overlooked for plum opportunities available to my peers,"* said a Black male lawyer. In architecture, 88 percent of white men said they develop design ideas, which is the most prestigious work. Only 61 percent of multiracial women reported having the opportunity to develop design ideas. *"I come up with all the work effort to prepare all the presentations and design, but I'm not invited to the presentations. I don't have the client interaction,"* commented a Latino. In architecture, only about a quarter of white men said they did more behind-the-scenes work than their colleagues, compared to nearly half of women of color. (White women and men of color were around 40 percent.)

Women of all races report not just less access to the glamour work but also more office housework. This can include literal housework (cleaning up the coffee cups, planning parties); administrative work (finding a time everyone can meet, sending the follow-up email); emotion work (mentoring, playing the peacemaker); and undervalued behind-the-scenes work. In academia, Latinas were the group most saddled with these tasks. *"I'm asked to be kind of the mother of the group. I play many roles that . . . could be done by a competent administrative assistant,"* said a Latina clinical science professor. *"I often get treated as a secretary by project leads that are older men. They have asked me to make meetings . . . to take notes . . . and I have even been asked to retrieve coffee from their desk, which they were upset about when I said no,"* said a woman engineer.

Experiments also show that women do more "organizational citizenship behavior"—like helping a colleague who is behind on a deadline—and typically get less credit for doing it.[37] That's because women are expected to be helpful and altruistic. "I'm like the friggin' firm mom. People come to see me if they're having problems," said a lawyer.[38] A woman engineer added, *"A woman can be forced to change jobs because they have the 'right' personality to deal with the difficult customer."*

In both law and architecture, white women reported doing more literal housework and administrative work than their colleagues, at rates two to three times those of white men (see figure 12-2). Rates of literal housework for multiracial women in architecture were five times as high as white men's (see figure 12-3). About half of women architects, but only a third of men, reported doing more emotion work than their colleagues.

Undervalued work can also mean poorer-quality projects. *"Women are given the bad projects. Men are given the juicy jobs,"* a Latina told us. *"All the projects which no one wants to do ended up on me somehow,"* reported an Asian American architect. A Latina architect's colleagues jokingly referred to her as "the public bathroom queen" because of her steady work of designing public bathrooms. *"The glamour work is managing clients who have had a large liquidity event or are still creating substantial wealth—the CEO or successful entrepreneur,"* said a woman in wealth management. *"Those opportunities often go to men, while women get stuck with the relatively smaller account of the little old lady who needs a lot of hand-holding and calls when she forgets her account password."*

A more subtle type of office housework is committee work in environments where no one gets promoted based on committee work. *"Three male colleagues . . . have never been asked to serve on any committees except ones directly related to their work, and most serve on one committee . . . I serve on the diversity committee, outreach committee, and safety committee. I have not seen a male even asked about serving on [these types of committees] in the eight years I have been at this research location,"* one white woman told us.

Diversity work is also often undervalued, as are mentoring and things like running the summer intern program. In tech startups, women often end up doing not only DEI but also all of HR, but then are assessed only on how they do the job they were actually hired for.

The end result is a double whammy. Not only do women get less access to the career-enhancing work; they also carry heavier loads of keeping-the-trains-running work. So if they do manage to get access to the glamour work, they need to work longer hours than men to make time for it. For more about this topic, see chapter 12.

Tightrope bias affects success at every job stage

Racial stereotyping and tightrope bias play out in many different workplace systems. Here, I'm just going to focus on penalties for assertive behavior. Addressing the tightrope dynamics that govern access to opportunities is so complex and crucial that chapter 13 is dedicated to it.

Hiring

Women sometimes find they can survive interviews only if they can deftly handle hostile questions white men rarely encounter. *"When a young woman professor showed some impatience in the face of some questioning after her job talk, this alienated some members of the department who opposed her candidacy. The leading male candidate showed similar impatience; no one even mentioned it."* This pattern, and the need to avoid it, should be discussed with anyone involved in interviews.

Performance evaluations

A 2020 study of tech evaluations found that 70 percent of comments that someone was aggressive were on women's evaluations, while 71 percent of comments that someone was too soft were on men's evaluations. Note, again, how bias pushes both men and women into their "proper" roles. The same study found that "taking charge" behaviors predicted the highest ratings . . . but only for men. Women were complimented for being helpful more often than men—but it didn't help either get top ratings. Finally, positive comments about one's personal work style predicted higher ratings for women, but not for men.[39] Having a positive personality seems more optional for men than women: our study of a Wall Street law firm found that women were penalized if they were not seen as warm. Men weren't.[40]

We have found similar patterns by race. In working with one firm, we saw that 91 percent of people of color, but only 77 percent of white men, had personal style mentioned in their performance evaluations; white women fell in between at 82 percent.[41] People of color were also dramatically more likely than white people to receive comments that they were "well liked" and had "a good attitude," suggesting that this was mandatory for people of color but optional for white people.

Women who deliver developmental feedback—a vital part of any manager's job—tend to be disliked and seen as less competent.[42] That's why 360-degree evaluations should be handled with care, as they can be rife with bias. If you do 360-degree evaluations—and they are a good idea—someone who understands what tightrope bias looks like should review them before they are finalized. Better yet, give a workshop on how to fill out an effective 360 and include information about bias.

Meetings

Tightrope bias plays out in meetings in ways that undercut women—especially those with expertise. Men with expertise tend to be *more* influential than men without it, while women with expertise tend to be *less* influential than women without it.[43] *"It often appears to me that [my] colleague values the more authoritative male's opinion over my own, even though I am supposed to be asked,"* said a woman engineer. Feeding this dynamic is the fact that displays of confidence and directness increase men's influence but decrease women's.[44]

Ignoring your experts can make them less likely to offer their expertise.[45] *"I brought up a flaw in a colleague's calculations, and when I argued for my point, I was labeled aggressive. Now I'm just bringing in baked goods and being agreeable,"* said a woman engineer.

For ways to interrupt bias in meetings, see chapter 15.

Interrupting tightrope bias

If your company is not actively searching for and controlling for backlash effects, they are probably happening. People in all roles need to be aware of backlash effects so they can stop applying different standards to different groups—and so they can trust the system if they are the ones being reviewed. This is one reason implicit bias training is important—but by itself, it's just not enough. Workplace systems should be structured in a way that makes backlash easy to spot. It needs to be safe for women and people of color to call out backlash. Otherwise, calling out backlash can just create more backlash.

In too many companies, white men of modest political talents can muddle through, while women and people of color need to have superstar-level savvy to keep up. A crucial step in fixing this imbalance is to separate two kinds of developmental feedback on performance evaluations: issues of personal style to be addressed and skills to be developed. Once these are in separate boxes (literally or figuratively), it's easy to look for demographic patterns. If you find them, hold a workshop—ideally, shortly before you begin your next performance evaluations cycle—on how common patterns of bias show up in evaluations.

To control for bias in interviews, find out whether women or people of color are getting judged on standards of niceness not applied to white men. Again, structure is important: the easiest way to do this is through a rubric that separates out personal style concerns from skill set concerns. But you may need to go further if you find that some groups are getting harried by hostile questions white men do not encounter. A 2021 study found that female economists get more questions, and more hostile questions, than men do.[46] Effective strategies to interrupt this dynamic, if it exists at your company, will be highly dependent on company culture. But I guarantee you one thing: if you don't interrupt that kind of bias, you will have persistent problems not only in recruiting candidates but also in retaining the talent you already have.

Trickier politics? That's not meritocracy

Suffice it to say that figuring out how to behave authoritatively in a way that doesn't make white people uncomfortable (if you are a person of color) or that doesn't make men uncomfortable (if you're a woman) is more difficult than just going for it without worry. Workplace systems should be structured to make that tightrope bias apparent. To learn how, see chapters 12 and 14.

Women and people of color should not be required to be ever-cheerful, never-demanding team players while white men are free to go for the gold. This requires creating an environment where double standards can be brought up and discussed. Otherwise, individuals who resist backlash can just face more backlash for being "difficult," "intimidating," or "touchy."

Making these changes will help everyone by sending a strong message to all levels of the organization—that when you say "meritocracy matters," you mean it.

CHAPTER 5

Are you saying that white men have it easy? I don't *feel* privileged

"As an older white male, I have faced significant reverse discrimination and find it very ironic that I'm told that I have some inherent advantage because of who I am. It's nonsense and the exact opposite of what I have been confronted with."

—White male engineer

The backlash against diversity is very real, though it varies a lot by industry. In our national surveys, engineers commented at a rate of over four times higher than lawyers that diversity was threatening the quality of their profession.[1]

Men in STEM (science, technology, engineering, and math) are more reluctant than women, and more reluctant than men in other fields, to accept evidence of gender bias.[2] The backlash in engineering reflects the view that engineering is highly meritocratic and "should be disconnected from 'social' and 'political' concerns because such considerations bias otherwise 'pure' engineering practice," found a study by sociologist Erin A. Cech.[3] Our surveys show that the backlash against diversity in engineering is much stronger than in law, though perhaps lawyers are just more careful about what they write down. DEI initiatives should assume backlash exists even if it is not openly expressed.

Sometimes, skepticism of DEI efforts reflects rank sexism. *"Diversity is overly emphasized relative to technical issues governed by physical laws . . . Woman managers are much more difficult to work for and with . . . They also tend to enlarge solvable problems into intractable issues,"* said a white male engineer.

But it's a mistake to think backlash is beneath the notice of top professionals. Some steps can help defuse it.

I can't tell you the number of times I have been teaching a bias workshop to a group of people who appear more fascinated by the songbirds outside the window than what's happening in the room—but once I start talking about the burdens bias places on certain groups of white men, they abandon their bird-watching careers, reorient their chairs, and listen up.

The class culture gap

Social inequality is the water we swim in, and it's important to capture all the currents. I've researched gender and racial bias for most of my career, but I have always worked on social class too, for a simple reason: I am a silver-spoon girl who married into a blue-collar family forty-three years ago, so I have spent my life bridging what I call the class culture gap. After the 2016 US presidential election, I spent two years talking nonstop about the white working class, including with an essay I wrote for hbr.org immediately after the election; it went viral and eventually became my book *White Working Class*.[4]

It's a mistake to talk about race and gender privilege without also talking about class privilege. That's a surefire way to alienate professionals who are the first in their families to graduate from college ("first-gen"). First-gen white men are often infuriated when they are depicted as privileged, because compared with white men from college-educated families, they aren't privileged in professional jobs. (In blue-collar environments, white men without college degrees are typically the dominant group, so dynamics are different.[5])

An extensive literature documents the pervasive influence of social class.[6] Kids like me were raised from our mothers' knees with the dispositions and skills valued in elite jobs. We were raised understanding that deft self-promotion is better than hiding your light under a bushel. We were raised understanding that you need to step outside your comfort zone of family and friends to develop an "entrepreneurial network" of weak ties to a broad range of people who can be useful as future clients, allies, and sponsors.[7]

People from nonelite backgrounds were raised with a different set of cultural values. Often their families look down on networking as the politicking of "shirt and tie types," aka "middle-class game-playing bullshit" (to quote two blue-collar men).[8] Blue-collar families typically look down on self-promotion, too, and place a higher value than elites on modesty and humility.[9] People from elite backgrounds are more comfortable with individualism, whereas those from blue-collar backgrounds tend to value community and solidarity more.[10]

This class culture gap translates into challenges adapting to, and navigating, white-collar environments and can create an "otherness" that inclusion initiatives need to address.[11] Class-based bias is less strong in technical fields like engineering than in fields like law, real estate investment, and banking, which depend more heavily on networking and cultural capital.

In a law firm we worked with, first-generation professionals reported the lowest levels of culture fit of any group (see figure 5-1). On many other measures, first-gen white men reported experiences more akin to those of women and people

FIGURE 5-1

The culture here is a good fit for me

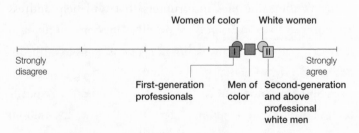

Note: "Women of color" and "Men of color" include all people who identified as Black, Asian or Asian American, Latinx or Hispanic, multiracial, or any other nonwhite option. The data for the "of color" group provides an average of the data for each specific group.

of color than to those of white men from college-educated families. This includes whether their ideas are valued when they talk in meetings, whether they have to work harder than other colleagues to receive the same level of recognition, and whether they have the same access to desirable assignments. In engineering, class differentials exist but are subtler.

Other research finds that first-gen professionals report lower levels of belonging and often feel disadvantaged by not knowing the "rules of the game."[12] Fully 97 percent of professionals from working-class backgrounds reported that their social class origin impacts their work experience.[13] A 2016 study found that over half of social class disadvantage was attributable to factors such as discrimination.[14] And yet a study of DiversityInc's 2019 list of the top fifty companies for DEI found that not a single one referred to social class in its diversity statement.[15]

Omitting class shoots your DEI initiative in the foot in two different ways.

First, you alienate white male professionals from blue-collar backgrounds who might otherwise be natural allies. Many of the same bias interrupters that will help address structural racism and sexism also will help them.

Second, a diversity initiative that fails to discuss the impact of social class will not be as effective in helping women or people of color as one that does. Some (though by no means all) of the isolation and exclusion experienced by people of color in professional-managerial roles stems from the fact that people of color are more likely than white people to be first-generation professionals. Nationwide, over half of first-gen college students are people of color.[16] So it's not surprising that a 2020 study found that class origins matter more for Black Americans than for white ones when it comes to attaining management positions.[17] Class also matters more for women: a 2021 study found that first-gen women are more disadvantaged than first-gen men.[18]

White men are not just packets of privilege

When discussing social inequality, it's important to remember that bias describes tendencies, not absolutes. Some white men report each of the patterns of bias described throughout the book: they feel they have to prove themselves repeatedly, their mistakes are hyperscrutinized, and so on. That doesn't disprove the existence of social inequality among different groups, but it's important to acknowledge that people are not just packets of social privilege, and life is not peachy keen for all white men. Bias describes social forces and how they affect individuals' lives. But every individual's life can be affected by personal challenges and psychological pain.

Another important step to help defuse backlash is to include age in your discussions of bias. In the quote that begins this chapter, the white male engineer in question identifies himself as "older." In our nationwide study, engineers aged fifty-five to sixty-four reported more prove-it-again bias than engineers under thirty-five. Engineers forty-five and older reported more bias in performance evaluations; engineers sixty-five and older reported more in promotions.

A typical comment: *"Some opportunities are not available if you're seen as older and have 'less runway.'"*

He may well be right, especially in engineering. If you were born in the 1940s or 1950s and studied engineering, you studied vacuum tubes—then shortly after college you needed to know about transistors, a brand-new thing with nothing in common with the tubes. Then you needed to learn about integrated circuits in binary logic—unrelated to transistors—and later, computer programming languages. And if you are not a cloud or mobile expert today, good luck keeping your job or getting a promotion. That's a lot of change in one career.

Stereotypes based on age have been extensively documented.[19] A review found fourteen articles documenting the stereotype that older workers have lower ability and are less motivated and productive; fourteen articles on the stereotype that older workers are harder to train, less adaptable and flexible, and more resistant to change; and ten on older workers supposedly having a lower ability to learn and therefore less potential for development than younger workers. The same meta-analysis identifies nearly seventy studies documenting that age stereotypes influence the outcomes of decisions in hiring, performance appraisals, and other business systems. Age stereotypes are particularly strong in computing, finance, insurance, and retail. All of this highlights the need to include bias based on age in DEI work.

Including age can help defuse backlash; so can pointing out that gender bias disadvantages many *men*. When gender stereotypes are allowed to flourish, not only will "difficult" women be disadvantaged for their failure to be sufficiently modest, self-effacing, and nice; modest and introverted men will be disadvantaged for being seen as insufficiently direct, assertive, or competitive. Modest men are also seen as having less leadership ability, ambition, and confidence.[20] In masculinity contest cultures, discussed in chapter 6, typically no woman wins, but most men lose too: both suffer from toxic leadership.[21]

The problem with gender stereotypes is they push both men and women into straitjackets. The "humility penalty" disproportionately affects groups brought up with a modesty mandate, including blue-collar men and Asian American men.[22] As one first-gen professional described it, *"In my family, admitting to ability or intelligence is a great sin and indicated that you were 'stuck on yourself.'"*

This discussion shows how easy it ought to be to talk about how the current system works poorly for many groups—including many white men.

Class bias affects success at every job stage

Bias based on social class affects professional-managerial employment in many different ways.

Hiring

One of my favorite experiments sent résumés with identical qualifications but different hobbies to elite law firms. Some listed elite hobbies like polo, sailing, and classical music. The others listed pickup soccer, country music, and mentoring other first-generation college students. Mr. Polo was twelve times more likely to get a callback; only 1 percent of the other men got a callback, because elite candidates were seen both as more competent and as a better fit.[23] That sends a cautionary message about hobbies on a résumé. Chapter 6 contains more on culture fit.

Probably the strongest source of bias based on class origin in most professional-managerial jobs is when students from a narrow range of elite schools are given artificial advantages.

For one year, I taught at Harvard. Having taught for most of my career in lower-ranked institutions, I was disoriented by all the recognition and deference I suddenly received from around the world. And then I realized: *This isn't about me—it's about Harvard. Don't let all the invitations go to your head. People now assume you're brilliant.*

Many companies use graduation from a narrow range of elite schools as a proxy for intelligence and a predictor of future success. This artificially advantages rich people: students from families in the top 1 percent are seventy-seven times more likely to attend Ivy League colleges than students from families in the lowest quartile of household income.[24] Yet a little-known fact is that students from lower-ranked schools are often as successful in the workplace as students from top-ranked schools.[25]

Nonelite students are much more likely to choose to attend a college close to home or a state school, or to start out at a community college and then transfer to a state university.[26] Educational path has little or no correlation with the quality of an employee in real life. That's why Google, which used to hire only from top universities, now hires from a much broader range of schools. Google also discovered another reason the Ivies aren't always the best bet: new hires from top schools were more likely to want to leave their jobs soon after starting.[27] "We now prefer a bright, hard-working student who graduated at the top of her class from a state school over an average or even above-average Ivy League grad," said Laszlo Bock, then the SVP of People Operations at Google.[28]

In addition, unpaid internships should not be overvalued because—obviously—students who have to find paid work can't afford to take them. It's important to recognize the drive and focus behind many first-gen students' ability to balance going to school with having a job that supports doing so.

Another way class privilege shapes hiring is that class elites tend to be more confident, or even overconfident, of their abilities as compared to those with less-elite backgrounds. A 2019 study found that elites tend to be overconfident and that this overconfidence often is mistaken for intelligence.[29] "Sometimes wrong; never in doubt" goes the joke about surgeons.[30]

To counter this, your company should send candidates a document explaining what qualities the company seeks—before they show up for the interview. This document should list self-confidence if it is highly valued. (An example of what this memo might look like is available at www.biasinterrupters.org.) The memo should say explicitly that undue modesty will not be helpful and that the candidates' assignment is to make the best case possible for themselves. This will counter the modesty mandate.

Performance evaluations and promotions

The modesty mandate can also affect evaluations that include a self-appraisal. To counter this, give employees explicit guidance on what the company would like to see in a self-evaluation. (We have a worksheet on writing an effective self-evaluation on www.biasinterrupters.org.) Clear instructions will encourage people from elite backgrounds to explain what justifies their confidence and will help ensure that first-gen professionals are not hobbled by modesty. It will also help other groups affected by the modesty mandate, like women and Asian American men.

Additional ideas

If your mentoring program is targeted to women and people of color, consider including first-gen white men too, particularly in industries like real estate, architecture, investment banking, and law. Employee resource groups have proved an important way for underrepresented groups to increase their sense of belonging, find others who share their experiences, and build skills. Consider forming a first-gen employee resource group to create community and build navigational competency. As with any employee resource group, some first-gen professionals would prefer to pass. No judgment.

A level playing field is level for everyone

What if you've done all that and there's still backlash? Don't back down. Remember that white men are still advantaged in high-level jobs: roughly 85 percent of corporate executives and board members are white men, a number that has not budged in decades.[31] White men are so dominant that it's almost funny: in 2015 there were four times as many CEOs named John, Robert, William, and James as there were women CEOs.[32]

Would your company abandon an effort to improve sales just because some people prefer not to get with the program? It would not. If you decide to abandon or gut your DEI initiatives due to backlash, you just learned something important about yourself: you actually didn't care about DEI. Employees aren't free to ignore or undermine other important business goals, so if they can ignore DEI goals, that speaks volumes about whether a company actually values DEI. To quote Tim Ryan, chair and senior partner of PwC, "Are there people who just feel like they got cheated? Yes there are. And what I say to those people is, 'I'm asking you to respect what we are trying to do. I'm asking you to respect our colleagues. I'm asking you to have compassion. And if you don't agree, that's OK. You don't have to agree with me. But I do need you to live our values.'"[33]

That said, also take steps to effectively communicate how a level playing field is level for everyone. As we will see in chapter 7, upgrading organizational systems to interrupt bias will help all groups, including white men. Leveling the playing field supports an organization's commitment to true meritocracy, will attract and retain quality teammates, and will reduce destructive dynamics in office politics—as the firms who have built bias interrupters deeply into their business systems will attest.

CHAPTER 6

We cherish our culture. Can we retain that and still achieve DEI goals?

"Vague terms such as 'she doesn't really fit in' and 'we just don't trust her' are often used to camouflage discomfort with someone of a nonwhite race."

—Woman of color, large STEM organization

Leaders obsess over their company cultures, and rightly so. A study by sociologist Lauren A. Rivera found that over half of those interviewed in law firms and investment banks rated culture fit as more important than analytical or communication skills.[1] More important for lawyers than analytical skills? That's important indeed.

Culture eats strategy for breakfast, to quote famed management consultant Peter Drucker.[2] I get that. The problems come when culture fit is used by people already at the company to ensure new people are just like them in ways that have little or nothing to do with business goals. Rivera's study found that culture fit often includes individuals' leisure pursuits, "people I can be buddies with," and "polish" and "presence." Leisure activities often include athletics, which can be problematic because some sports are heavily male; many require extensive time and expense and so are heavily exclusionary by race and social class. *"Anyone who plays squash, I love,"* said one banker.[3] If you are using squash as a job requirement, you aren't interested in diversity. Same goes for the "lunch test": hiring only those you'd like to have lunch with. It's pleasant to find friends at work, but if you're hiring only mini-mes you are by definition not hiring for diversity.

The problem with "polish" is more subtle. In some jobs, polish doesn't matter: the unpolished theoretical physicist will likely be as successful as the polished version. In jobs where bonding with people is super important, people skills are essential. But be careful not to conflate people skills with a certain style of polish that's class-specific. Again, anything that's class-specific will have exclusionary effects by race as well as class.

If you use culture fit as a requirement at your company, make sure your definition of it is limited to workplace dispositions and habits, which you should be able to articulate. Rivera's study shows how appropriate culture-fit criteria are often intermixed with inappropriate ones: *"You want someone that makes you feel comfortable, that you enjoy hanging out with, [who] can maintain a cool head when times are tough and make tough times kind of fun."*[4] The last two are work-relevant character traits; the first two are friend-relevant and will have exclusionary effects if applied at work.

"You've got this male circle going on. They all golf together, they all fish together, they are a clique," said a white woman in a company in a rural area. Again, if the goal is to hire mini-mes, you pay a price. While research shows that people on diverse teams typically feel less comfortable than people on nondiverse teams do, it has also found, as will be discussed in chapter 15, that well-managed diverse teams outperform homogeneous ones.[5]

The most famous kind of culture fit is "Googleyness," defined by Laszlo Bock, Google's former SVP of People Operations, as: "Attributes like enjoying fun (who doesn't), a certain dose of intellectual humility (it's hard to learn if you can't admit that you might be wrong), a strong measure of conscientiousness (we want owners, not employees), comfort with ambiguity (we don't know how our business will evolve, and navigating Google internally requires dealing with a lot of ambiguity), and evidence that you've taken some courageous or interesting paths in your life."[6] This is a good example of a work-relevant definition of culture fit. (Google insists "Googleyness" does not mean culture fit, but by any definition, it is.[7])

So if culture fit is important to you, clearly define the attributes you truly care about—not just one manifestation of them. Look for an outgoing person rather than a frat boy. Look for a an intense nerd rather than a fan of your favorite subreddit. Assess whether someone has the disposition of a fighter pilot, rather than whether they literally were a fighter pilot. (The latter is a common test for culture fit in higher levels of the US Air Force.)

The remainder of this chapter describes three ways culture fit can be misused to create companies that are exclusionary by race, gender, or social class.

The teddy bear effect

Cultures rife with racist insults and stereotypes need not detain us for long. It goes without saying that such cultures will require a sustained change initiative that begins with a clear setting of boundaries, including communicating that such insults and stereotypes will not be tolerated. That kind of behavior is illegal and can lead to large legal judgments and harsh reputational effects.

More-subtle behavior can have exclusionary long-term consequences. Consider the teddy bear effect. A 2009 study by Robert W. Livingston and Nicholas A. Pearce found that white CEOs typically have mature-looking faces, while Black CEOs are typically baby-faced. Black men with strong jaws or fierce demeanors likely don't get to lead companies, because white people feel too threatened by them; Black CEOs were also seen as warmer than white ones. Baby-faced Black leaders are emblematic of workplace cultures where people of color, and especially Black people, cannot thrive without racial comfort strategies.[8] This makes Black males "more constrained in their leadership [as] compared with white males," conclude Livingston and Pearce.[9]

This is, of course, a form of tightrope bias: white men just need to look and act authoritative in order to get ahead, but people of color need to establish their authority in ways that are nonthreatening to white people, which is far trickier.

Culture fit also can have exclusionary effects by race and gender. While only half of white male architects have left or considered leaving their firms due to a lack of fit, nearly three-quarters of women of all races and two-thirds of men of color have. White male architects overwhelmingly feel they can do their best work, but only about two-thirds of Black women do. White men are also much more likely to see a clear path for advancement (see figure 6-1).

FIGURE 6-1

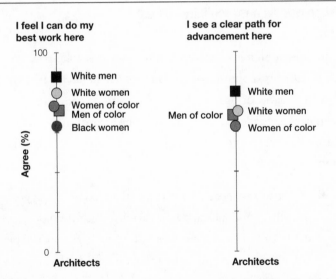

Note: "Women of color" and "Men of color" include all people who identified as Black, Asian or Asian American, Latinx or Hispanic, multiracial, or any other nonwhite option. The data for the "of color" group provides an average of the data for each specific group.

Where available, the graphs highlight the group whose experiences diverge the most from white men's. When a single group is not highlighted, the percentage differentials between the individual groups were too small to be meaningful.

More-subtle teddy bear problems are reflected in who is "well liked." As noted in chapter 7, our study of performance evaluations found that people of color were much more likely than white men to have comments that they were well liked (57 percent versus 40 percent) and had a good attitude (67 percent versus 46 percent). The teddy bear effect was strongest for Black men: 83 percent were praised for having a good attitude, versus 46 percent of white men. On the one hand, having people who are well liked is a plus; on the other, if being well liked is more mandatory for people of color than for white people, that's racism.

When work is a masculinity contest

Equally problematic are corporate cultures where work is a masculinity contest. *Masculinity contest cultures* enshrine a specific strand of peacocking as the coin of the realm. Researchers have identified four basic elements of such cultures, which are correlated with each other and with organizational dysfunction:

- **"Show no weakness"**: workplaces that demand swaggering self-confidence and that caricature admissions of doubt or tender emotions as "sissy stuff" (or much worse language used around the watercooler or in the gym).[10]

- **"Stamina and strength"**: workplaces that prize displays of strength and athleticism. In white-collar companies that don't involve manual work, this takes the form of spending extreme hours at the office and engaging in extreme sports outside it.

- **"Work devotion"**: workplaces that define commitment as being always available for work (i.e., having immunity from family responsibilities because someone else is taking care of them).

- **"Dog-eat-dog"**: Machiavellian workplaces dominated by "mine's bigger than yours" competition where zero-sum thinking divides colleagues into "winners" and "losers."

Masculinity contest cultures corrode company effectiveness in three distinct ways. The first is encouraging unreasonable risk-taking (physical risk-taking in blue-collar jobs; financial in white-collar jobs). Second is making braggadocio and endless social dominance contests, which deflect attention from shared business goals to personal power grabs, the norm. Third is expecting extreme hours as a display of work commitment, even though they aren't the unmitigated windfall employers often assume. (More about that in chapter 9.) Our study of women of color in tech found that masculinity contest cultures were highly correlated with all five patterns of bias, and with worse outcomes for women of color: lower intent to stay with one's employer; less career satisfaction, belonging, and engagement; and a higher sense of being stalled in one's career.[11]

Researchers have developed a validated scale of masculinity contest cultures. The box provides some simple questions to tip you off if you have a problem. (This is an abbreviated version of the full scale, which can be found in the source cited.[12])

Organizations that score high on the scale tend to have leaders who abuse and bully others and high levels of racial harassment, sexual harassment, and social humiliation.[13] These organizations also tend to lack psychological safety, which makes colleagues reluctant to "put themselves out there," point out problems, share new ideas, or tackle stretch

Does your company have a masculinity contest culture? To find out, use the following survey items. Ask people whether they agree with the following statements:

- Admitting you don't know the answer looks weak.

- Expressing any emotion other than anger or pride makes you look weak.

- It's important to be in good physical shape to be respected. People who are physically smaller have to work harder to get respect.

- To succeed, you can't let family interfere with work.

- Taking days off is frowned upon.

- You're either "in" or you're "out," and once you're out, you're out.

- If you don't stand up for yourself, people will step on you.

assignments.[14] Sky-high levels of work-family conflict make it difficult to retain anyone who isn't married to a stay-at-home spouse. These organizations also have higher rates of burnout, turnover, illness, and depression among both male and female employees.

The first step in changing a masculinity contest culture is to recognize that many people, men as well as women, don't endorse it. After all, in environments where there is only one "top dog" and everyone else is a "loser," nearly everyone is defined as a loser. People generally overestimate the extent to which others endorse masculinity contest cultures.[15] Everyone feels like they're the only one who's unhappy. The upside is that these cultures turn out to be fragile once they are effectively challenged. If a few brave people point out that the emperor has no clothes, many more are likely to agree.

Sex, drugs, and angry young men

Even companies that don't have a full-on masculinity contest culture may have a culture that revolves around drinking, drugs or sex. By now, we've all read the articles exposing inappropriate behavior at WeWork and Uber. No company wants that kind of reputation.

People drink with their colleagues for a simple reason: it's a way to loosen up and build bonds. In Japan, for example, work colleagues often are expected to go out drinking with the boss and engage in drinking games.[16] In Japan and many other places, drinking games can devolve into masculinity contests in which strength and stamina are measured by your ability to hold your liquor.

"After the meeting, they all went out for beer and things got pretty informal. I felt uncomfortable and excluded." A company culture that revolves around drinking puts women in an impossible position. It's one thing for a group of men to bond over beers, but when a woman goes out boozing with them, it's a no-win situation: either she's uptight and a buzzkill, or she out-guys the guys—and gets judged for that.

The best way to level the playing field is to send a consistent message that drinking to excess is inappropriate in any professional context. Post-#MeToo, employers don't want to be in the position of having a jury decide whether they were creating a hostile work environment where sexual harassment was prevalent.[17]

Keep in mind that many people—men as well as women—feel uncomfortable when there's pressure to engage in excessive drinking. To quote one white man, *"Due to my religious affiliation and no interest in sports, I'm very much left out of the good-old-boy network—drinks and golf games."*

Sex talk at work also puts women in an awkward position. If they join in, they may well be seen as inviting sexual advances. If they don't, they may well be seen as frigid and no fun. Women are disadvantaged when there's sex talk at work even when they say that they enjoy it.[18]

Finally, if your company culture condones lashing out in anger, there's probably a pattern as to who's allowed to do it. Open expressions of anger tend to increase the perceived status of a man but decrease the perceived status of a woman.[19] As we've seen, often people of color are perceived as angry even when they're not, and showing anger is far riskier for them. Research shows that women and people of color are subjected to selective incivility that increases the likelihood they will leave their organizations.[20] The simple solution is to adopt, publicize, and enforce an anti-harassment policy that includes civility requirements and the message that such displays of anger are not acceptable and that employees can and will be disciplined for them.

When golf is a work requirement

Remember Mr. Polo from chapter 5? People who grew up around country club types feel comfortable with golf and tennis; first-gen college students are less likely to, so they will get left behind if golf's a requirement for promotion. So will many women: women are less than one-fourth of all golfers.[21] "'A man's gotta golf'—a quote from my manager after gathering the male engineers from my meeting so they could tee off at 2 p.m.," said a female colleague. Women also are less likely than men to have someone else be responsible for their kids after work hours, even if they do golf. For any white male executive at a loss as to why golf might feel exclusionary, imagine if your boss came to a meeting and said he was taking the department to a spa day. Would you feel like you belonged?

This doesn't mean you need to stop bonding with clients over golf; that ain't going to happen. But if a good chunk of the crucial networking—with people inside the company or outside it—takes place on the golf course, companies need to provide alternative opportunities for networking that are less heavily race-, gender-, and class-linked. Alternative activities will depend a lot on context, but here are some evergreens: going to a sports event or a concert, taking a bike ride or hike (OK, I'm from California), engaging in volunteer social service work, or playing online games and activities.

In addition, sponsors need to bond with their protégés in ways that aren't exclusionary. We heard of a powerful executive who bonded with protégés by going running, complete with crucial conversations held in the men's locker room. That's a good way to have women leave the company. I've already quoted the woman who noted, *"You've got this male circle going on. They all golf together, they all fish together, they are a clique."* Think about whether your company's style of sponsorship only works for certain groups. *"This up-and-coming male . . . they're patting him on the back . . . he knows all the details of the bosses' lives. It wouldn't be appropriate for me to do so,"* said one woman.

Class is expressed through cultural differences, not just how much money is in your bank account.[22] Everything from the way we dress, to the food we eat, to the way we raise families, to what we do on the weekends is influenced by social class.

In elite workplaces, first-gen professionals find themselves constantly "covering" any indication of their class and social background to fit in, avoiding mentions of things that might mark them as part of a different social sphere, like that great family meal they had at Olive Garden, or how their uncle, or they, voted for Donald Trump.[23]

Covering means changing your appearance, behavior, and attitudes to fit into the mainstream. It means avoiding any behaviors that are stereotypical of working-class people and not standing up to the casual classism of coworkers: a colleague unthinkingly describing a reality TV star as "white trash" or a certain restaurant chain as "redneck." People of color have to cover a lot; first-generation professionals of color may have to do it even more than first-gen white people. No matter who you are, covering is taxing, tiring, and isolating.

A civil and professional corporate culture helps everyone

Be as disruptive as you want in achieving your business goals, but remember: business is about teams. People have to feel that they belong in order to do their best work. To achieve this, most companies won't need a culture reboot; just civility and professionalism, with some reasonable boundaries on "fun," consistently required across the board.

CHAPTER 7

Can we make progress on DEI without getting all rigid and bureaucratic?

"Organization scholars since Max Weber have argued that formal personnel systems can prevent discrimination."

—Frank Dobbin, Daniel Schrage, and Alexandra Kalev

Sometimes I divide the world into jazz and classical musicians. Classical musicians are emblematic of people who like everything pinned down and perfect. Jazz musicians are emblematic of those who like to improvise and go with the flow. This difference is captured by the preference for "openness" in the Big Five personality test, or the "judging" versus "perceiving" vector of Myers-Briggs.

You may be worried that getting better at DEI means your company will go from a culture of innovation and creativity to one of stuffy, ossified compliance. That's not true, as the case study in this chapter will show. But we first need to understand a basic truth: organizations without structure run on defaults—and defaults subvert DEI goals for reasons that go deep into human psychology.

An organization that runs on default defaults to homophily

Take a minute to picture who is at the top levels of your company. Next, exclude the head of HR, the DEI lead, and the general counsel—leadership positions more likely to be held by women and people of color. Of those remaining, how many are white men from college-educated families? It may be close to 100 percent.[1]

Network homophily is a fancy name for a simple truth. Like likes like: the single strongest determinant of who is in your default network is similarity.[2] So an organization where white men from college-educated families predominate at the top will tend to promote other men just like them.[3] *"They make sure their golden boys are the next generation of leaders,"* said a frustrated woman engineer. The golden boys get privileged access to sponsors, inside information, and valued assignments. And here's the thing about golden boys: they're usually golden, and they're usually boys.

Referral hiring

Referral hiring, or hiring through alumni networks, will tend to reproduce the existing racial, gender, and class breakdown of the company. If that's your goal, keep on keepin' on. If not, keep track of whether the referral/alumni stream disproportionately favors one group. If it does, either eliminate it or add additional channels to make the recruiting pool more diverse. These additional channels typically will be either affinity-based professional groups or institutions that serve groups underrepresented at your company. We often hear that recruiting from these channels "takes too long." Actually, it doesn't take any longer once you have established relationships. As for the time needed to develop those new relationships . . . is your company willing to make some investments in order to achieve DEI goals? If not, then I guess they're not important goals. Would you balk at an up-front investment in the new sales tool that will help you achieve your sales goals?

Access to opportunities

Informal processes, like tap-on-the-shoulder promotions, channel opportunities to whoever's top of mind. So does what the military calls "hey you" tasking—making assignments based on whoever happens to be around. The result is the same people get tapped again and again, and others get left out despite their talents. We have worked with companies where women don't advance because valued assignments are passed out in lunches to which only the in-group of white men is invited. Evening out access to opportunities is not an easy problem to solve, so it's discussed in two separate chapters. Chapter 11 details how CEOs can broaden access to opportunities; chapter 15 details how individual managers can.

Sponsorship

Sponsorship is integral to getting opportunities. (A sponsor is more than a mentor; it's someone who is willing to spend their own political capital to help their protégé advance.) If your company isn't requiring managers to keep track of whom they are sponsoring, I suspect, alas, that white men at the top are chiefly sponsoring other white men just like themselves. A simple way to ensure that sponsorship does not go overwhelmingly to one small group is to have people submit whom they are sponsoring to a central database and look for demographic patterns, and then train the sponsors on how to widen their circle of protégés. The more robust way is to institute a formal sponsorship program, described in chapter 12.

Compensation

Women and people of color get paid less than white men with similar performance evaluations.[4] We hear comments like this one over and over again:

> *I feel it is very difficult to have a successful career as a female attorney working at a law firm that has been part of the "good old boys" network for many years, particularly in a Southern state. I am expected to work harder than my male colleagues and I do not get paid as much as they do, compared to the volume of hours I bill and the volume of clients (and business generally) that I generate for the firm.*

Regression analysis shows that women attorneys and attorneys of color with the same metrics as white men still get paid less.[5] And gender pay gaps, which persist across industries, are hardly a secret. Bill Maher, a popular comedian who was hoping Hillary Clinton would win the 2016 US presidential election, joked that "we could pay her less for the same job" as one more reason people should vote for her.

Prove-it-again bias plays a role in pay gaps, as do "good old boy" network effects. In one study, 32 percent of white women law firm partners, and 36 percent of women partners of color, reported being "bullied, threatened, or intimi-dated" out of claiming origination credit.[6] (The lawyer with origination credit pockets a hefty percentage of the client's billings.) White male lawyers were twenty-four percentage points more likely than white women, and thirty-one per-centage points more likely than women lawyers of color, to say that their pay was comparable to that of colleagues with similar experience. A big part of the problem is a compen-sation system where origination credit is negotiated infor-mally and in private. If that's how your compensation works, be sure there's an appeals process that people can use without being perceived as "whining."[7]

Compensation bias is an easy problem to check for: it's just a math problem. Look at whether there are demographic patterns in compensation that are not explained by seniority and ratings. Do it under privilege with outside counsel if you are concerned about this data being used against you, but you should at least know where things stand. Plenty of companies have done the math, and the more courageous ones are completely open about it. Salesforce is famous for its proactive approach: in 2018, it followed up its analysis by spending $6 million to increase salaries of women.[8]

Case study: Notching up the formality without creating stultifying bureaucracy

Because so many companies and people fear that the only alternative to unbridled discretion is stultifying bureau-cracy, it's worth looking at a case study in detail. At first glance, the vast majority of the evaluations at one company seemed useful and appropriate, with few obvious problems. But when we coded the evaluations and looked for patterns in the actual words, we found that race and gender strongly influenced them. We reviewed 3,603 evaluations in year one and 717 evaluations with 3,585 comments in year two.

Most dramatically, in year one only 9.5 percent of people of color had leadership mentioned in their performance evaluations (seventy percentage points lower than white women). People of color were also far less likely than whites to have promotion mentioned (24 percent versus 35 percent). Evaluations of people of color were almost twice as likely as white men's to mention mistakes (43 percent versus 26 percent). All this suggested prove-it-again bias.

Clear evidence of tightrope bias emerged too. Over 90 percent of people of color had personal style mentioned in their evaluations, as compared with only 77 percent of white men. More tightrope bias: 50 percent of Black women's evaluations included mentions of doing the undervalued, behind-the-scenes "office housework," compared to 16 percent of white women and 3 percent of white men. The evaluations also suggested the teddy bear effect: nearly 60 percent of people of color, but only about 40 percent of white people, got comments that they were "well liked"; nearly 70 percent of people of color, but only about half of white people, got comments that they had a "good attitude."

White women faced some of the same challenges, and some different ones. Almost 20 percent of their evaluations had comments suggesting that those women didn't want to make partner. We suspected this was driven by maternal wall bias. We also found evidence of tightrope bias: 27 percent of white women, but only 10 percent of white men, were praised for being "friendly and warm."

This firm did not give global ratings before it started working with us, but we found that women received more positive comments than men in performance evaluations. White women were wildly more likely than white men to have leadership mentioned (82 percent versus 43 percent); they were also more likely to have positive comments, be called a value or asset, have their mistakes written off as not their fault, and have proactive behavior and other positive aspects of personal style mentioned.

Despite all these positives, white women's supporters worried they weren't getting their due: *"I believe she is a key player in our group and encourage the committee to consider her for a generous raise."* The evaluations also suggested that white women needed to be willing to sacrifice more than white men. Women were nearly twice as likely as men (22 percent versus 12 percent) to get comments about being overworked.

Small, evidence-based changes can have big effects

To address these and other challenges, we worked with the firm to implement two bias interrupters. First, we changed the evaluation form. The original form did not specify what competencies the organization valued or require evidence to justify the ratings. The new form broke job categories down into specific competencies, and asked that ratings be backed by at least three pieces of evidence.

We also helped the company develop a simple, one-hour workshop that taught people how to use the new form as well as showed comments from the prior year's evaluations and asked a simple question: which of the five basic patterns of bias does this comment represent, or does it represent no bias?

In other words, we made the performance evaluation slightly more "bureaucratic"—but not a lot more. The results were dramatic.

People of color got more leadership mentions in year two—and such mentions predicted performance ratings. They also got wildly more constructive feedback. Only 17 percent of the comments given to people of color were constructive feedback in year one, as compared to 49 percent in year two. Constructive feedback increased for white women (11 percent to 30 percent) and white men (15 percent to 27 percent) too.

Creating more evidence-based workplace systems helps every group

Let me highlight a supremely important point: the new evidence-based system *helped every group—including white men*.

The new evaluation form's specificity had concrete business benefits. For one thing, it allowed for more-effective assessments of skills that were of great value to the firm, notably contributions to client development and client approval. The firm identified "taking initiative" as a core value and identified it as a competency on the form, and then saw a dramatic increase in the number of employees who received a comment describing a time they took initiative. The change was most dramatic for people of color (from 19 percent in year one to 94 percent in year two), but it was significant for white people too. In addition, negative personal style comments about people of color sharply declined in year two: 14 percent had such a comment in year one; the next year, none did.

Most important, when the company shifted to focusing on specific skills and competencies, white men lost their unearned advantage over people of color in promotion recommendations. White women remained more likely than white men to have a promotion mentioned in their evaluations: either they have an artificial advantage that has persisted, or they were underleveled and needed to be promoted.

In sum, the intervention helped white men by giving them more-constructive feedback, helped other groups by leveling the playing field, and helped the organization achieve its business goals more effectively. With that payoff, even a jazz musician can tolerate a bit more structure.

Women's priorities change after having kids. Are you saying I should ignore that?

"Women get pregnant. This is a real disadvantage and risk for any project leader . . . So given the same qualifications, I would rationally go for the man. Not saying it's right, just saying there are logical reasons behind it."

—Public comment left in response to a study showing a candidate named "John" was more likely to be hired than an equally qualified "Jennifer"[1]

Here's the short answer: the fact that some mothers cut back on work after they have children does not justify discriminating against them, or against the women who don't.

Motherhood triggers the strongest form of gender bias

I've already mentioned the study by sociologist Shelley Correll and coauthors that found that mothers are 79 percent less likely to be hired, only half as likely to be promoted, and are offered an average of $11,000 less in salary than women with identical qualifications but no children.[2] Mothers also are held to higher performance and punctuality standards. Studies documenting other aspects of maternal wall bias date back nearly twenty years.[3]

The Correll experiment also compared résumés of a father and a man without children and found that the father was *more likely* to be hired and promoted, was offered $4,000 more in salary, and was held to lower performance and punctuality standards than a man with identical qualifications but no children.[4]

There's a well-documented wage penalty for mothers and wage premium for fathers: she's seen as less committed and competent because her priority is her family, the faulty logic goes; he'll work harder because he has a family to support. Interestingly, the motherhood wage penalty has all but disappeared for high-income mothers, but women are still losing ground because the fatherhood wage premium has increased sharply for high-earning men.[5] No need to highlight how fundamentally unfair this is to women with children and men without. Bias hurts everyone.

Our survey research finds that only about half of women, but around 80 percent of men, report that having children didn't cause colleagues to question their competence and commitment. Women of color report maternal wall bias at nearly the same level as white women (see figure 8-1).

In architecture, Latinas are nearly three times more likely than white men, and nearly twice as likely as white women,

FIGURE 8-1

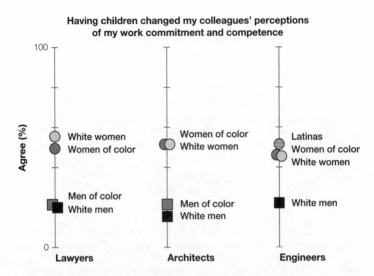

Having children changed my colleagues' perceptions of my work commitment and competence

Note: "Women of color" and "Men of color" include all people who identified as Black, Asian or Asian American, Latinx or Hispanic, multiracial, or any other nonwhite option. The data for the "of color" group provides an average of the data for each specific group. We did not receive enough responses from male engineers of color to draw conclusions.

Where available, the graphs highlight the group whose experiences diverge the most from white men's. When a single group is not highlighted, the percentage differentials between the individual groups were too small to be meaningful.

to report colleagues have said that mothers should work less. Women in architecture are twenty-one percentage points more likely than men to say that taking family leave would hurt their careers; in law and engineering, the divergences are smaller but still substantial (see figure 8-2). This is all the more striking given that penalizing someone for taking family leave is illegal in the United States under the Family and Medical Leave Act.

FIGURE 8-2

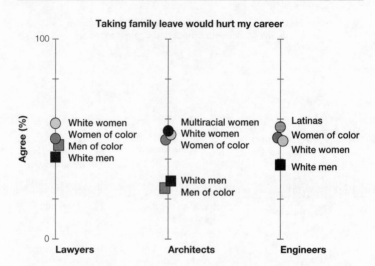

Note: "Women of color" and "Men of color" include all people who identified as Black, Asian or Asian American, Latinx or Hispanic, multiracial, or any other nonwhite option. The data for the "of color" group provides an average of the data for each specific group. We did not receive enough responses from male engineers of color to draw conclusions.

Where available, the graphs highlight the group whose experiences diverge the most from white men's. When a single group is not highlighted, the percentage differentials between the individual groups were too small to be meaningful.

Not surprisingly, we hear a raft of comments about the many flavors of maternal wall bias in our surveys:

> *People would say in pitch meetings, "She has four children,"
> as if she was a Flying Wallenda or something, and she
> would get very irritated. "Why are you talking about my
> children? Why aren't you talking about my competence?"*

> *My colleagues assume I am a slacker because I have chil-
> dren, even when I come in on the evenings or weekends to
> make up time that I have to miss due to my children.*

*Not getting a raise or paid equally with my male peers
right after getting back from maternity leave; there was a
perception that as a new working mother, I wouldn't be
able to put in the same effort.*[6]

Maternal wall bias means that, when mothers return from
maternity leave, they often have to start proving themselves
all over again: it's prove-it-again squared. Mothers also walk
a tightrope between being seen as bad mothers because they
are too committed to work, and being seen as bad workers because they are too committed to family. "I get that
a lot: 'Don't you feel bad leaving your kids at home? Don't
you miss them?' And I say, 'Sure, I miss them. My husband
misses them too, but I have a wonderful relationship with
my kids; my children are fabulous.' And they say, 'Oh, my
wife could never do that, never leave the kids,'"[7] said an
Asian American woman lawyer. Note the message: a good
mom would not do what you do. One experiment found
that successful mothers are seen as less likable than successful
fathers, are held to higher performance standards, and are
penalized on hiring, promotion, and salary.[8]

The same message often is delivered benevolently, as
when a manager fails to offer a plum assignment to a new
mother: *"This new manager told me directly that I would not
'want' a promotion because it requires more responsibility, and I am
a mom so I wouldn't want to travel."* Different tone of voice,
but the message is the same: a good mom wouldn't want it.
Please take your lack of opportunity as a compliment!

Caregiver discrimination is prohibited by US federal
law.[9] And it may be easy to litigate because people are often

loose-lipped about their outdated expectations of mothers, and older men frequently make negative comments when younger men request family leave. Plaintiffs win in two-thirds of cases brought in federal courts, a dramatically higher success rate than in most other types of employment discrimination cases.[10] Paying attention to caregiver bias is more than just the right thing to do.

The flexibility stigma affects both women and men

Maternal wall bias may also be triggered when a woman goes part-time or adopts a flexible schedule. *"We have great workplace flexibility programs on paper, but there can be an unwritten stigma associated with using them,"* one woman wrote in a typical survey comment. This is so common it even has a name: *flexibility stigma.*[11] Obviously, if a woman is working 80 percent, she will be paid only 80 percent. That's not a problem—but paying her 70 percent is. And obviously, if someone is working 50 percent, she may take longer to get promoted since she's accumulating promotion-related experience at a slower rate. That's not a problem—but barring all part-timers from promotion is. That includes making part-timers promotable in theory but not in practice. *"I spent fifteen-plus years putting in unbelievable hours, pushing myself to near burnout for this company prior to having a baby,"* wrote one woman who had dropped down to thirty-five hours after becoming a mother. *"They don't come right out and say there's a problem, but the 'vibe' is there, and lately I've been worried about how secure my position is."* I often wonder if she ended up losing her job.

If many employers pressure women out of breadwinner roles, they also pressure men out of caregiver roles. As noted already, having children helps men's careers—but only if they signal someone else is in charge of their children. Men who request family leave are viewed as higher on "feminine" traits (i.e., weaker and more uncertain) and lower on "masculine" traits (i.e., less competitive and ambitious), one experiment found.[12] Another found that men and women value workplace flexibility equally, but that men may be reluctant to request a flexible schedule due to fears that others would see them as less masculine—and that men who asked for a flexible schedule anyway were indeed seen as less masculine.[13] Men who requested workplace flexibility were seen as less competitive, less committed to their careers, and lower in leadership potential. They were, in short, seen as poor workers—a flexibility stigma that was fully explained by the fact they were perceived as more feminine than other men: the flexibility stigma is really a femininity stigma.

This means that the flexibility stigma is sex discrimination.[14] As one man told us, *"When I inquired about parental leave, people were surprised. 'We expect your wife will do it.'"* Note that penalizing anyone for taking parental leave—male or female—is illegal in the US under the Family and Medical Leave Act.[15]

Another dynamic employers need to be attuned to is generational clash among men. A prominent example was the dustup that occurred in 2014 when Mike Francesa (b. 1954), a sports show host, criticized the New York Mets' Daniel Murphy (b. 1985) for taking the three-day paternity leave negotiated by his union. "You're a Major League Baseball player," said Francesa, "you can hire a nurse. What are you gonna do, sit there and look at your wife in the hospital bed for two days?" MSNBC host Chris Hayes (b. 1979) sprang to Murphy's defense: "Take some time with the partner in your life who brought the kid into the world . . . That actually is part of *being* a man." This tug-of-war among men ties back to identity threat. The older men feel attacked because they feel like the younger men are accusing them of being bad fathers. When cherished identities are attacked, things get ugly fast.

To retain women, ask whether men take parental leave

When companies tell me that they are committed to retaining women, the first question I ask is whether the *men* are taking their full parental leave—not two days or two weeks, but leaves as long as their female colleagues take. Here's the logic:

- Given that 78 percent of college-educated women have children, a company won't be able to retain a proportionate number of women if it can't retain mothers.[16]

- You won't retain mothers if leave is stigmatized.

- The best way to tell whether leave is stigmatized is whether men take it.

QED: If you want to retain women, make sure men take their full leave.

Employers should offer full leave to men not just to retain women, but also to retain men: 72 percent of millennial men, but only 59 percent of baby boomer men, say they would take a full three months' paid paternity leave if it was offered.[17] Again, among millennials, men and women value flexibility equally highly, and rank flexible working hours as the second most valuable benefit their employer can offer (after training and development).

For many, the assumption that young men and women value flexibility equally defies common sense. That's because when women leave due to prove-it-again bias and tightrope bias, they often tell employers they are leaving for family reasons—because they are ambitious and don't want to burn bridges. When men leave for family reasons, they often say it's for a better offer—because they are ambitious and don't want to burn bridges. Each group gives accepted gendered reasons, which leaves employers understandably convinced that women care about work-life balance and men don't. But many men do, and you should assume that if those at your company don't take family leave, it's because they know it's not allowed—and you can assume that men are leaving to join companies more compatible with their values. (They're not telling you this, I know. But they tell me.)

Women without children are also affected by maternal wall bias

Women without children can encounter maternal wall bias too if it's assumed they will have kids at some point. In fact, women without children report the highest levels of workplace mistreatment, including bullying.[18] They may be seen as slightly pathetic types with "no life," in a modern version of the "spinster" stereotype. So stereotypes surrounding motherhood affect all women, whether or not they have children.

Maternal wall bias affects success at every job stage

By now, it should be clear that just knowing bias exists isn't enough to overcome it. So too with maternal wall bias. Here's how it plays out in three core business systems:

Hiring

Managers (both men and women) are sometimes surprisingly frank in admitting bias against women of childbearing age, at least behind closed doors. One typical comment: *"We've interviewed young women, and people will say, 'Yeah, but will she be here at nine months from now?' so it does influence hiring."*

Many companies also look askance at a gap in a résumé. This will knock some women out of consideration because many do take time off for child-rearing—and highly qualified women are the most likely group to do so.[19] Someone who's out for a year or two for a baby still has market-current skills—not to mention new expertise at handling many different demands at once on little sleep. Just as companies accommodate military personnel who have deployments, they should accommodate mothers, because companies' long-term future depends not only on safe national borders but also on the next generation of citizens, consumers, and employees. Behavioral economists Joni Hersch and Jennifer Bennett Shinall found that women fare better when they explain a gap in their résumés; give her a chance to explain rather than pretending to ignore it.[20]

Access to opportunities

Two-thirds of women in architecture say that women's opportunities diminish after they have children.[21] When these women leave because their careers have stalled, firms may assume they're leaving because "their priorities have changed." We hear similar stories from women in engineering. *"I felt very 'mommy-tracked,' assigned to low-profile work, less-interesting projects, and little customer interaction. This is part of why I left that company two years ago and found a role with a new company that's been much more flexible and respectful of my role as mother and engineer."* Another woman engineer had a very different experience: *"I have been afforded great flexibility here for my four children and have been very appreciative that this has not diminished my assignments or influence at work."* Which of these very different experiences do women have at your company? With some thoughtful preparation and disciplined implementation, you can get it right.

Another common problem is when women with reduced schedules are relegated to dead-end work—or no work. *"Went on reduced work schedule due to having kids—and suddenly could not get [work]. Basically, I have been forced to leave,"* said a white woman lawyer. This is not inevitable. Every job consists of bundles of different tasks; supervisors need to get analytical and not assume that a bundle of tasks that traditionally have gone together can't be rethought.

Supervisors should receive training that tells them that if they have a stretch opportunity that's time- or travel-intensive, they should offer it to parents, not just nonparents. But tell fathers as well as mothers, "If this isn't a good fit right now, don't hesitate to say so; these things come around from time to time, and I'm happy to tell you the next time something does."

Then make sure you do.

Fair pay and promotions

"I wanted to apply for a promotion position as an assistant director, but was told by the hiring manager not to bother, as I would not be selected because I was going on maternity [leave for] six to eight weeks," said a white woman. *"I asked why I got a raise that was below average when my performance review showed my work exceeded or highly exceeded expectations, and I was told it was because I went on maternity leave for eight weeks,"* said another woman at a large company. To reiterate: it is illegal to retaliate against someone for taking parental leave; the

Family and Medical Leave Act says so. The law requires you to treat parents in exactly the same way as if they had never taken leave.

Interrupting maternal wall bias

To make the workplace work for parents and nonparents alike, the first step is to send a strong message that comments and assumptions about someone's childcare responsibilities have no place in hiring decisions, performance evaluations, access to opportunities, or promotions. A second message is that employees should check at the office door their personal assumptions about the best way to run someone else's family life. Tolstoy was wrong—happy families are not all alike.

The third step is to send the message that men as well as women are expected to take their full parental leave. This means giving equal parental leave to men and women, instead of "primary caregiver policies" that give a substantial leave to the primary caregiver and a millisecond to the secondary caregiver. We hear all the time that millennial fathers are baffled by these policies: *"I don't get it. We are equal caregivers."*

Primary caregiver policies are outdated—and legally risky if everyone knows that they are for mothers and that fathers aren't supposed to use them. All it takes is one person to say so explicitly, and you've got a lawsuit on your hands.

The final step is to set up a formal process so people can transition seamlessly onto and off of leave. Both mothers and fathers need this. As one white man told us, *"I took parental leave while my son was an infant, and I felt that the organization failed to work with me to develop a good transition plan so that I would have projects to work on when I returned to work full-time."*

A three-meeting protocol is in order. As soon as a pregnancy is announced, the leave-taker's direct supervisor or department head should meet with the employee, congratulate them, and identify what work can be completed before the leave (be realistic) and what work will need to be transitioned. The next step is to solicit ideas for whom to transition that work to—making it clear this is input only, and that it is up to management, not the leave-taker, to develop a successful transition plan. Obviously, this timeline will need to be adapted for adoptive parents.

The second meeting should occur about a month before the leave starts. This meeting will pin down a transition plan and discuss the leave-taker's current thoughts about their schedule upon their return—thoughts that might change. Ideally, the company should have a gradual-return-to-work policy that automatically allows leave-takers to return on a reduced-hours basis and gradually work up to full-time. Otherwise, people with unreceptive managers may face an overwhelming wall of work upon their return, and end up leaving the company as a result.

The third meeting should take place on the employee's first day back at work after leave ends, to communicate the plan for reintegration. Weekly meetings for the first few weeks or months will help ensure a smooth transition.

A final element of a best-practice leave policy is to make it available to all forms of family caregiving, including elder care. Remember that family forms differ, particularly in the LGBTQ+ community and communities of color, so don't restrict caregiving leave to parents and children.

Our worksheets on identifying and interrupting bias in hiring and performance evaluations, found on www .biasinterrupters.org, can help interrupt maternal wall bias.

Don't worry about keeping mothers—worry about keeping workers

Inevitably, this chapter has focused mostly on mothers, but keep in mind that it isn't just women who need time for life outside the office. It's fathers too, but it's also a wide range of other people, including older workers who care for ailing spouses. Remember, too, that people of color and first-gen professionals tend to have caregiving responsibilities for a wider range of kin than white professionals from college-educated families do—not only their immediate family, but also the granny or auntie who raised them or the *comadre* who cared for them.[22]

And while caregiving is important, it's not the only reason that, over the course of a lifetime, people need time off—others could be divorce, or poor health, or any number of life events. I sometimes joke that it would be far more convenient to just hire a workforce of robots. We're not there yet—and I wouldn't want to be. Would you?

CHAPTER 9

Isn't it natural—and inevitable—that people who work harder go further?

Not really. A recent randomized controlled trial showed that always-on work cultures are in fact counterproductive—and that individually negotiated flexible work arrangements aren't the answer.

Led by Erin Kelly and Phyllis Moen, the experiment worked with teams, not individuals. Researchers helped teams talk through how best to get their work done without overload and burnout. They also helped them rethink how to minimize low-value work, how to be responsive to real deadlines without treating everything as equally urgent, how to communicate both availability and project updates, and how to implement the Results-Only Work Environment (which measures results while letting employees decide when and where to work). These four elements they called the STAR intervention (Support, Transform, Achieve, Results).[1] The experiment implemented this plan with one group, while a control group continued work as usual.

The results of the STAR intervention were dramatic, even if the sample size was small. Neither work nor work-loads changed, but employees in the intervention group reported lower levels of burnout and higher job satisfaction than did the control group. And employees in the STAR group left the company at a 40 percent lower rate, with retention higher among the experienced workers (typically the most valuable). Again, this was despite the fact that employees in the intervention group *did not work fewer hours*. So if you're a manager or a CEO, why would you *not* adopt STAR? Your people could be working the same number of hours and be a lot happier. STAR will likely save on labor costs because attrition is expensive. Typically, it costs a minimum of 30 percent to 150 percent of an employee's annual salary to replace them when they leave, and for professionals the costs can be much higher in lost productivity, recruiting, onboarding, and training.[2]

But so few companies do this. Why?

Maybe because we are still stuck in the 1960s paradigm of work, with a fixed time and place, fixed roles, fixed beliefs about who does what when. It's time to listen to the new data. Time and again, work redesign studies show great results, and time and again, successful interventions are abandoned, perhaps because employers reassure themselves that work-life balance is just a women's issue—even though men report higher rates of work-family conflict than women do.[3]

Consider the example of a midsize global consulting firm that hired three prominent researchers to investigate why the firm was unable to retain women. They found that men and women had virtually identical turnover rates, and that men were as likely as women to say that work interfered with their family lives due to a 24-7, always-on, travel-at-the-drop-of-a-hat work culture. The researchers proposed to change the firm's practice of overselling and overdelivering, a practice related more to social display than client needs. One consultant described "slide decks that take hours and hours of work. It's this attitude of 'I'm going to kill the client with a one-hundred-slide deck.' But the client can't use all that! People do it so others on the team will see they're smart."[4]

All of this went unheeded. The firm ignored the researchers' findings, ended the study, and implemented programming for women. Other successful initiatives were abandoned as well.[5] Why does this keep happening?

Work, identity, and purity

For professional-managerial men, ambition and a strong work ethic are "doubly sacred . . . as signs of both moral and socioeconomic purity," to quote sociologist Michèle Lamont.[6] Elite men's jobs revolve around what sociologists call the *work devotion schema*, which dictates that high-level professionals should "demonstrate commitment by making work the central focus of their lives" and "manifest singular 'devotion to work,' unencumbered by family responsibilities," notes sociologist Mary Blair-Loy.[7] This ideal has roots in the seventeenth-century Protestant work ethic, in which work was viewed as a calling to serve God and society. The religious connection has vanished . . . or has it?

Blair-Loy notes that the words she heard from professionals in law and finance are those often used to describe ecstatic religious devotion—"complete euphoria" or "being totally consumed." "I worshiped my mentor," said one woman. "Holidays are a nuisance because you have to stop working," said another banker. "I remember being really annoyed when it was Thanksgiving. Damn, why did I have to stop working to go eat turkey?" One confessed to missing a favorite uncle's funeral, "because I had a deposition scheduled that was too important."[8]

Work devotion is performative. When I was a visiting professor at Harvard Law School, I called it the cult of busy smartness. "I am slammed" is a socially acceptable way of saying "I am important." Fifty years ago, Americans signaled social class by displaying their leisure: think bankers' hours (9 a.m. to 3 p.m.). Today the working rich display their extreme schedules.

Not only is work devotion a "class act"—a way of enacting class status—it's also a certain way of being a "real" man.[9] Working long hours is seen as a "heroic activity," noted a study of lawyers.[10] Marianne Cooper's study of Silicon Valley engineers captures how pencil pushing is turned into a test of manly physical endurance: "Guys try to out-macho each other, but in engineering it's really perverted because out-machoing someone means being more of a nerd . . . It's not like being a brave firefighter and going up one more flight than your friend. There's a lot of 'See how many hours I can work,' whether or not you have a kid . . . 'He's a real man; he works ninety-hour weeks. He's a slacker; he works fifty hours a week."[11] At a consulting company, the always-traveling consultants referred to themselves as "road warriors"; at a hospital, the always-on surgeons called themselves Iron Men.[12] All this, of course, is work as a masculinity contest. Notice the Silicon Valley engineer's competition with blue-collar men ("brave firefighter").

"Successful enactment of this masculinity," Cooper concludes, "involves displaying one's exhaustion, physically and verbally, in order to convey the depth of one's commitment, stamina, and virility."[13] She found men who described a lack of effective delegation and widespread exhaustion. Silicon Valley fuels this ethic by providing employee benefits that reinforce the ideal of a worker with no life outside of work, who eats three meals a day at the office, gets their dry cleaning and haircuts there, and satisfies their spiritual yearnings through meditation classes on the company campus.

The STAR study documents the pain men felt at their attenuation from family life—and also how many men protect themselves from feeling that pain by convincing themselves that (real?) men don't really mind, only women do. "I just think mothers have a different kind of bond with their children," opined one male at the consulting firm.[14] But for many men that just wasn't true. "I was traveling three days a week and seeing my children once or twice a week for forty-five minutes before they went to bed. Saturday came, and I couldn't go to my son's soccer game. He burst into tears. I wanted to quit then and there," said one. Said another, "Last year was hard with my 105 flights. I was feeling pretty fried. I've missed too much of my kids' lives."[15]

It's all Kabuki theater: Erin Reid's study of management consultants found that men who weren't always-on ideal workers but *pretended* to be received slightly higher ratings than men who actually were always on. But men's evaluations suffered if they openly rejected the ideal-worker model.

Note that men who worked less got *higher* performance ratings—yet another demonstration of the business case for family-friendly policies, which has been documented again and again.[16] But the business case fails to convince because what's at issue is not money or productivity; it's deeper—it's about cherished identities. Men who have missed their children's childhoods have a lot invested in believing that extreme schedules are the only way to get the work done. Workaholic women have to fit the stereotype as well.

The ratcheting up of working hours is a relatively recent phenomenon and dominates only in male-dominated occupations.[17] In the 1970s, people who worked more than fifty hours a week suffered a wage *penalty* of almost 10 percent. By the end of the 1990s, 40 percent of managerial men worked more than fifty hours a week, and they enjoyed a 10 percent wage premium.[18] Some of this may have to do with the fact that any hours over forty are not paid as overtime, but instead are lumped into an amorphous, evidence-free "annual bonus."

This overwork effect is so strong that it wiped out women's gains from increased educational attainment.[19] Long-hours work cultures significantly increase the likelihood of attrition among mothers.[20] In other words, just as women flooded into highly paid high status jobs, those jobs' time norms shifted to create terrain on which it was impossible for women to compete.

A long-hours culture sabotages diversity goals

So here's where we stand. The brute fact is that organizations where full-time is more than fifty hours per week will struggle to retain and advance a proportionate number of women, because only *12 percent of college-educated women work more than fifty hours per week.*[21]

This is blazingly obvious; what's less obvious is that always-on work cultures also drive out many men. Millennial dads are more likely than older men to believe that being a good father requires more than being a "good provider"— it requires being involved in children's daily care. If they can't realize that ideal, many will follow the mothers out the door. Always-on cultures assume that the ideal worker has someone else caring for their children, which is especially difficult for single mothers. This has a racial effect: two-thirds of Black children have single mothers.[22]

One reason it's hard for leaders to bend their minds around this issue is their own family arrangements are so unusual. While two-thirds of married Americans are in two-income households, and nearly 40 percent of all mothers are primary breadwinners, the breadwinner/homemaker family persists in one group: the top 1 percent of earners.[23] Fully 71 percent of these men have stay-at-home spouses.[24] Executives need to recognize that they manage a workforce whose family arrangements are very different from their own.

Changing a long-hours culture is challenging, but it's not impossible. Implementing STAR would be a lighter lift today because so many companies have experience with nearly everyone working remotely. This scale of remote work was unthinkable—until we all suddenly started doing it in March 2020. And it's been a success: 83 percent of employers said that Covid-related remote work is going well.[25] With remote work often comes workplace flexibility; many people are now used to taking time off during the day to attend to family matters and working flex time as needed.

Normalizing remote and flexible work is worth the trouble. A rigorous randomized controlled trial by economist Nicholas Bloom and his colleagues found that remote work enhanced performance by 11 percent—which improved to 22 percent when the company opened up remote work to all employees and allowed people choose remote or on-site work.[26] Another longitudinal study found that companies with "trust-based working hours" have 12 percent to 5 percent more product innovation and 6 percent to 7 percent more work-process innovation than other companies.[27] You have to trust your workforce to let them work remote.

During the 2020 pandemic, many companies that didn't believe they could function with remote and flexible work made a happy discovery. They could.

If we hire more women and people of color, won't the DEI problem take care of itself?

"Is you gonna be satisfied with a bone somebody done throwed you when you see them eating the whole hog?"

—Levee Green, *Ma Rainey's Black Bottom*

In his play, *Ma Rainey's Black Bottom*, August Wilson highlights intense conflicts within Rainey's all-Black backup band over whether one musician or another is too smiley and deferential to her white manager.[1] *One Night in Miami . . .*, a play by Kemp Powers, explores a similar theme, highlighting the conflict between Malcolm X and singer Sam Cooke over whether Cooke's success represents selling out to white people or triumphant Black (economic) Power.[2] (Both plays were released as movies in 2020.)

That's the tug-of-war—when bias against a group creates conflicts within it—and it's why hiring a few more people of color or women won't make your diversity problem magically disappear. Expecting women or people of color to champion members of their own group may be unrealistic— not to mention unfair—because championing diversity can be costly for those who step up. A study of 362 executives found that women and people of color who often signaled that they valued diversity were rated by their bosses as *much* lower in competence and performance than counterparts who didn't. Diversity champions were seen as less competent when they hired someone like themselves . . . except when the champions were white men.[3]

Again and again, we hear in our work with companies that workgroups headed by white men tend to give valued opportunities to other white men, while workgroups headed by women or people of color distribute such opportunities across all groups, including white men. These anecdotes are backed up by fifteen years of studies documenting the tug-of-war.[4] In effect, in-group favoritism doesn't work the same way for other groups as it does for white men. In architecture, about half of women reported conflicts with women, over three times the rate reported by white men. About a third of people of color reported conflicts with people of color, twice the rate reported by white men. Black architects and Asian American men were the most likely to report such conflict; nearly half did.

In-group favoritism combines with homophily to give white men privileged access both to sponsorship and to inside information. For example, in our study of architects, half of Black women felt left outside of informal information-sharing networks—but only one-fifth of white men did. Only a quarter of white men reported that there were unwritten rules they didn't know, compared with about half of white women, women of color, and men of color.[5] White male architects overwhelmingly (89 percent) said they knew what it takes to succeed at their organizations, but only two-thirds of Black women did (see figure 10-1).

Instead of in-group favoritism, women and people of color (and probably LGBTQ+ people, though I'm not aware of research on that) often encounter tug-of-war bias. That's

FIGURE 10-1

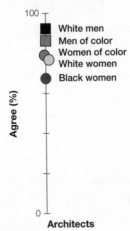

I know what it takes to succeed in my organization

■ White men
▦ Men of color
◐ Women of color
◯ White women
● Black women

Agree (%)

Architects

Note: "Women of color" and "Men of color" include all people who identified as Black, Asian or Asian American, Latinx or Hispanic, multiracial, or any other nonwhite option. The data for the "of color" group provides an average of the data for each specific group.

Where available, the graphs highlight the group whose experiences diverge the most from white men's.

when women are pitted against other women ("queen bee syndrome") and people of color are pitted against other people of color (aka "crabs in a barrel").

It's important to note up front that neither is inevitable or invariable. When we surveyed science professors, 76 percent of women said that female colleagues typically support each other: *"The [older] women . . . are always very encouraging, very helpful, and very kind."*

Problems arise when women and people of color are tokens—one of the few members of their own group, alone in a sea of white men. *"There is a definite white boys' club here. And even some of the women that were able to make it, they have the attitude of 'Suck it up, buttercup. I went through it too, so you have to go through it.'"* Studies show this happens for both women and people of color.[6]

Why don't other groups favor their own group in the same ways white men do? This has been discussed the most in the context of "queen bees" who target, rather than support, other women. This name is problematic because it implies that the problem is (yet again) with women's personalities; the research shows that tugs-of-war stem from bias against a group that creates conflict within the group.

A race discrimination case provides a dramatic example. The plaintiff, Shirdena Twymon, complained that at Wells Fargo objective rules were applied more rigorously to her than to white employees (prove-it-again bias) and that she was expected to act excessively deferential because she was Black (tightrope bias).[7] She was directed "to be accommodating and nice"—a mandate that didn't apply to her white colleagues. Phil Hall, the Black director of employee relations, told her that "intelligence and outspokenness in Black employees is not welcomed" and that "qualities that would make a Caucasian a golden child," such as "being aggressive and intelligent and outspoken and a go-getter, would do exactly the reverse to a person of color."[8] Twymon said that Hall advised her to develop a deferential persona as a "good Black" who "would be accepted by the Caucasians at Wells Fargo." She responded by asking if she should be an Uncle Tom. She was fired and then sued for race discrimination.

Similar conflicts arise among women. "I'm not a girl at Google, I'm a geek at Google," said tech executive Marissa Mayer when she worked at the internet search company. Note how adeptly she distances herself from the out-group (women) and aligns herself with the in-group (geeks). When work is a boys' club, some women join up, aligning with men against other women. Or they at least keep quiet: *"I know she didn't like the things that were going on, but she accepted them and refused to stand up in any way or even admit, publicly, that there was a problem,"* said one white woman of a colleague. Tug-of-war dynamics can also make women reluctant to participate in women's initiatives. *"I've heard that a lot. Women don't want to be associated with our women's group. They want to stay at arm's length because they don't want to be seen as 'one of those complainers.' Instead they align with the men."*

Studies show that some women do tend to align with men against other women.[9] This doesn't prove that they are wicked queen bees. It just shows that they are ambitious professionals operating in an environment of gender bias.

(Note that conflict among women tends to be pathologized, while conflict among men is seen as healthy competition—another insistence that women be selfless and not ambitious.[10])

The common assumption is that members of out-groups will advocate for others of their group; sometimes they do and sometimes they don't. In order to prove their value to their workgroups, women and people of color may align with the majority against their own group. People of color of all genders, for example, may be first-gen professionals who are concerned about job security because they lack a safety net. Out-group members often fear that advocating for others of their group will look like favoritism (*favoritism threat*): one study found that only 10 percent of professionals of color advocated for a "demographically similar other," but close to 40 percent of white men did so. White men advocating for other white men are often assumed to be doing it based on merit, because white men are assumed to be competent; women and people of color do not enjoy the same assumption of competence, so their advocacy may well be seen as unfair favoritism.

Out-group members also face a double bind: if there's room for only one (or a few) of their group to advance, and someone else is perceived as better than they are, they may lose out (*competitive threat*). *"Opportunities for women are very zero-sum. If one woman gets a prized position . . . another woman won't. And so it breeds a sense of competition,"* said one woman. Over a quarter of women engineers of color, and one-fifth of white women, reported that they have to compete for one "women's spot." Our study of women scientists found Black (32 percent) and Asian American women (30 percent) are sharply more likely than white women (17 percent) and Latinas (22 percent) to say they felt they were competing with other women for the "women's spot."[11]

But at the same time, if a member of their group is perceived as a poor performer, other women and people of color may be seen as incompetent by association (*comparison threat*).

Gender bias also is passed along from woman to woman. One study of legal secretaries found that half didn't care whether they worked with men or women.[12] But among those with a preference, not one legal secretary preferred to work with women lawyers. One explained it this way: *"Females are harder on their female assistants, more detail-oriented, and they have to fight harder to prove themselves, so they put that on you."*[13] Notice how the prove-it-again bias experienced by her boss fueled conflicts with this secretary.

Our research showed that women lawyers were twice as likely as white men to say that they did not get the same level of admin support as their colleagues (despite the fact that most admins are women). In architecture, people of color reported substantially more pushback from admins than white men did (despite the fact that admins at many companies are more likely to be people of color). We find similar patterns in industry after industry, with underrepresented people and Latinas the most affected (see figure 10-2).

All this make sense. If admins look up and see a sea of white men at the top, they may well conclude that it makes more sense to hitch their future to a white man. Women

FIGURE 10-2

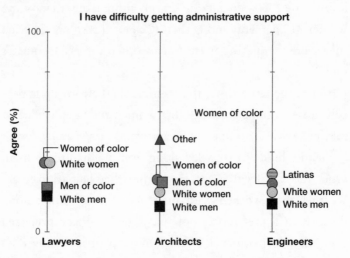

I have difficulty getting administrative support

Note: "Women of color" and "Men of color" include all people who identified as Black, Asian or Asian American, Latinx or Hispanic, multiracial, or any other nonwhite option. The data for the "of color" group provides an average of the data for each specific group. "Other" includes other underrepresented people. We did not receive enough responses from male engineers of color to draw conclusions.

Where available, the graphs highlight the group whose experiences diverge the most from white men's. When a single group is not highlighted, the percentage differentials between the individual groups were too small to be meaningful.

professionals also report that admins expect them to be more understanding than men, especially of work-family conflict. In other words, admins enforce gender stereotypes: men are expected to be competitive, ambitious, and direct, but women are expected to be interpersonally sensitive and emotionally supportive.

Maternal wall bias, too, can be passed from woman to woman. Older women sometimes fault younger women for going part-time or taking long maternity leaves. I'll admit it—I sometimes think: *I worked full-time my whole career, and my kids are fine.* (Note: I don't say this to anyone, and instead give myself a talking-to; that's the cognitive override I mentioned earlier in the book.) Older women judge other women, who judge them right back: *"I don't want to be an absent mom. I want to raise my own kids."* Ouch, that stings—my kids may be fine, but I was a bad mom by that standard. When the ideal worker and the ideal mother are defined as being mutually exclusive, most women end up judging each other: "You're a bad worker," one says. "Thanks, you're a bad mom," the other replies.

The term for these dynamics is *identity threat,* and it can be triggered by tightrope bias if women fault each other for being too masculine ("What a bitch! No wonder no one likes her") or too feminine ("With that little-girl voice, no wonder no one takes her seriously").

Race also enters in. White women often assume a female solidarity that women of color don't feel. As noted above, about three-fourths of women in one study felt that women usually support each other, but only 56 percent of Black women agreed.[14] In architecture, underrepresented people are the most likely to report pushback from admins. Among science professors, Latinas were particularly likely to report pushback: *"There is this Mexican woman telling them what to do,"* said one such scientist.

White women can act racist in the same ways white men do, but some patterns are gender-specific. One scientist reported *"feedback about being an empathetic person and how important it would be to try to make people more comfortable with me. I also think that part of what has been interpreted as my hard edges are attributable to me being a Black woman."* White women policed into femininity may do the same to Black women.[15]

Interrupt tug-of-war bias

The first step in interrupting tug-of-war bias is to recognize that, if relationships are freighted among women or people of color, it's probably a symptom of bias in their environment, not a sign that someone has a personality problem. The second step is to make sure there is not just one "women's spot" or "diversity slot" for highly coveted opportunities; that's a recipe for creating workplace conflict among groups that may already feeling embattled. The third step is to make sure that being a diversity advocate is not a costly career move at your company. Research suggests that the best way to accomplish this is to have white men take the lead in implementing and communicating these concepts.[16]

But the single most important message is that the best way to eliminate the tug-of-war is to eliminate the bias that gives rise to it. That leads us to the crucial role of the CEO.

CHAPTER 11

What does the CEO need to do to finally deliver on DEI goals?

Many CEOs are understandably frustrated. US companies spend roughly $8 billion a year on DEI initiatives and have little to show for it.[1] Those that idealistically posted their diversity metrics online are now publicly embarrassed by their lack of progress.

Here's the bottom line: Your business systems and climate reflect the people you've already hired. So if you want to replicate that workforce in the future, keep doing what you're doing. But if you really want to make progress toward your DEI goals, my reassuring message to CEOs is that you already know what to do. Just use the same tools you would use to solve any business problem. Begin with the evidence, use metrics to establish baselines and measure progress, and keep at it in a disciplined manner, using an iterative process until you achieve your goals. That's the new DEI playbook—and it works.

You have already made a good start by reading this book. Now that you know what bias looks like, and how it affects virtually every workplace system, you can readily see that what's needed is more than "woke washing"—the term for when companies announce they wish to dismantle bias or structural racism but don't actually make meaningful changes. Figure 11-1 and the graphs in chapter 1 show the pervasiveness and scope of the problem.

Across industries, women and people of color are eleven to fourteen percentage points less likely than white men to think performance evaluations are fair. White men are roughly fifteen to thirty percentage points more likely to feel that pay and opportunities for advancement are fair, with women of all races and Black men vying for the most dissatisfied group. White men are fourteen to twenty-one percentage points more likely than any other group to feel that hiring is fair.

Addressing structural racism and sexism requires changing structures. If you had a serious problem with your supply chain, you wouldn't try to solve it with a heartfelt email. This chapter presents a six-step protocol for the kind of structural change that's needed to actually deliver on your DEI goals, based on our experience and an overwhelming amount of data both old and recent.

Step 1: Give someone the authority and resources they need to solve the problem

Researchers Frank Dobbin, Daniel Schrage, and Alexandra Kalev found that two of the most effective interventions were appointing a diversity committee and hiring diversity

FIGURE 11-1

The pervasiveness of the lack of fairness problem

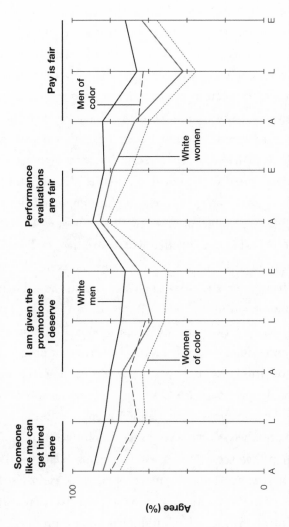

Note: L = lawyers, A = architects, and E = engineers. The lines in the graph for male engineers of color are incomplete where we did not receive enough responses from them to draw conclusions.

staff.[2] No surprise there. If it's not someone's job, it doesn't get done.

But I've hired a chief diversity officer, I hear you say. That's a good first step, but there's a structural problem at most companies. Again, to address systemic racism you need to change systems, and most chief diversity officers (CDOs) don't own the business systems that need to be changed. At many companies, HR owns performance evaluations and sees the business through an ops lens rather than a strategic lens. At many companies, recruiting is its own department. And in virtually all companies, neither HR nor DEI has authority over who gets access to plum opportunities or how performance is incentivized by line managers.

You can't engage in effective culture change if you splurge on a head of DEI who is competent and well-meaning but has little or no authority to change the business systems that create the culture.

Usually, DEI heads are given a budget to establish employee resource groups and offer enrichment programming. I know this because they hire our team and people like us to help. We give a great workshop, they pay us lots of money, and everyone goes away happy. Except me. Because I know it's very likely that nothing real is going to happen. This is a recipe for the same, if not bigger, problems—partly because your workforce is more aware and (rightly so) more demanding and empowered to ask for a level playing field.

Putting on capacity-building programming designed to increase the skills of women or people of color is never a bad thing. But it will solve your diversity problem only if the problem is that women and people of color lack capacity. It virtually never is. Typically, the issue is with your business systems, which are constantly transmitting well-documented forms of bias day after day, week after week, year after year.

So the first step is to give the CDO authority to do an audit of your basic business systems, including hiring, performance evaluation, access to opportunities, and compensation (and perhaps more—this is a minimum). This audit should use evidence-based process metrics to measure whether, and how, bias is creeping into each of these systems. If it is—and if you have a problem with diversity, that's likely—then the CDO needs influence *and the power* to have functional business leaders collaborate with them to redesign the business systems that need tweaking. Too often today, CDOs do not have this authority. Yet no one would expect to fix a problem in sales without giving the head of sales the authority to change policies and practices. Influence is not enough. And they can't just come back to you and report—this will tend to cause others on the executive team to treat them with suspicion. The role's purpose is not to spy on who is doing what. Set your CDO up to win.

The business leaders know the business; the CDO knows DEI. Both need to work together to effectively modify the systems without adverse impacts on business results. One analogy is thinking about the processes used by chief compliance officers: the CCO conceptualizes the approach and leads the charge, but the business leaders must own the results.

Obviously, this requires both more power and more influence than the typical chief diversity officer has. That is precisely why so much money has been spent with so few results. The answer is not to throw money at the problem, but to take a thorough, thoughtful, sustained approach.

Appointing a diversity committee can be even more effective than only hiring diversity staff. Alexandra Kalev, Frank Dobbin, and Erin Kelly found that such committees were associated with a 30 percent increase in Black women in management, a 14 percent increase in white women, and a 10 percent increase in Black men.[3] Why were diversity committees so effective? Since the study is an analysis of US Equal Employment Opportunity Commission data, we get little description of what these diversity committees were or why they worked. The organizational change literature, however, provides one.

John Kotter notes that effective organizational change almost always includes a guiding coalition to lead the way; the diversity committee can lead that coalition. A diversity committee should include some people who are powerful and some who are influential, typically because they are either central nodes in their networks or brokers who provide the link between different networks. Serving on the diversity committee should be a plum assignment, not "one more thing to do"; one way to ensure that is to have the committee report directly to the CEO.

Committee members should be receptive to DEI goals; they don't necessarily have to be advocates, but they must be willing to carefully collect and consider the evidence and then follow it. Also, needless to say, the responsibilities of the diversity committee should be defined as being part of someone's job and assessed in their performance evaluations. Otherwise, this is just another form of office housework.

The diversity committee should include white men, both for reasons of influence and to avoid loading this important and challenging change management work onto groups that are already disadvantaged by the lack of diversity. One good way of accomplishing all this is to designate the diversity committee an action learning team. We will talk more about that in the next chapter.

Step 2: Treat diversity as a business goal

If diversity is a core business goal, and it should be, treat it like one. The three basics: document why DEI is a business goal; use metrics to measure baselines and measure progress; and hold people accountable for achieving DEI goals, just as you would any other business goal. Then, promote the message with the troops, as you do with other initiatives. Explain to people in plain language why DEI is good for everyone, good for the bottom line, and good for shareholders. You can start by saying that your customer base is diverse, the world is shrinking, and the company is missing out on the creativity, resourcefulness, and productivity that diverse teams demonstrate in study after study, on many different metrics.[4]

Tie diversity goals to your core business goals. As an example, Erby Foster, the visionary diversity head at Clorox, explained how increasing diversity would help the company open up new markets for its consumer products. He mobilized employee resource groups (ERGs) to participate in a preexisting annual innovation contest at which anyone could pitch a new product or business idea. (Note that I have not discussed ERGs because so many companies already do them well.)

Before Foster took over, Clorox had embraced the conventional wisdom that marketing campaigns that would reach whites also would reach Asian Americans. Under Foster's guidance, the Asian-American ERG contested that. He armed it with consumer data, which enabled it to argue that Clorox was leaving lots of money on the table by not marketing explicitly to Asian Americans. The CEO personally tasked the ERG with finding a fix, and the group proposed buying the condiment company Soy Vay; that and subsequent acquisitions increased Clorox's sales to consumers of Asian-inspired condiments and sauces. These early wins were widely publicized and helped show the business case for diversity. Note how different this is from standard business–case data about how much greater companies' earnings are if they have more diversity. This is *specific information about how diversity helps an individual company achieve its most cherished goals*, in this case increasing market share. It took two to tango—the CDO to come up with the initiative based on his expertise and the CEO to keep the ERG accountable and spread the magic.

Another Clorox example: For decades, its Kingsford charcoal packaging had depicted "Barbecue Bob" on a red, white, and blue package—a white guy in a chef's apron evoking July 4. Erby armed the Latinx ERG with data about the outsize role of Latinx consumers; so armed, the group proposed new packaging with the red, white, and blue jersey of a popular Mexican soccer team, along with a marketing campaign to match. Sales of charcoal to Latinx consumers shot up, along with overall sales of meat, chicken, side dishes, and beverages commonly served at barbecues.

Show it, don't say it: specificity is the key to establishing the business case for diversity. Depending on your industry, some examples could include:

- **Consumer products/customers.** Show how diversity can enhance your company's ability to connect with customers, as Clorox did.

- **Tech/innovation.** Tech companies' AI proves downright embarrassing when it reads African Americans' faces as those of gorillas.[5] Perhaps that's an unfair outlier to highlight, but the literature on bias and algorithms is huge. In tech and other industries where innovation is important, a study of 4,277 companies in Spain found that those with more women were more likely to introduce radical new innovations over a two-year period.[6] Another persuasive argument was that tech companies rely on skilled workers from abroad, and "we want to be sure they are welcomed," found Kalev and Dobbin in a forthcoming study.[7]

- **Federal contractors/contracts.** For federal contractors, and that's a *lot* of companies, the most powerful message may be that diversity can enhance the firm's ability to get federal contracts. Kalev and Dobbin found when a company had a federal contract, all of the potential adverse effects of bias training disappeared, and were replaced by positive effects for Latinos and Asian American men.[8]

- **Venture capital.** Venture capital firms that increased women partner hires by 10 percent averaged a 1.5 percent increase in overall fund returns per year and had nearly 10 percent more profitable exits (which is pretty impressive, given that only 29 percent of all VC investments have profitable exits). Racially homogeneous teams reduced an investment's success rate by about 26 percent to 32 percent.[9]

- **Finance.** One experiment that placed financially literate people in either homogeneous or racially diverse teams found that diverse teams were 58 percent more likely to price stocks correctly.[10] A 2003 study of 177 national US banks found that, in innovation-focused banks, racial diversity enhanced financial performance.[11]

- **Whatever's the coin of the realm.** More generally, the business case for diversity at your company needs to link diversity with whatever is the coin of the realm. In law firms, it's profits per partner. In architecture, it's probably winning design competitions or prestigious commissions. The brass ring varies from industry to industry, but the key is to provide evidence that—whatever the ring is—a successful DEI initiative can help you grab it.

In any company, the most powerful business case is one that shows—not tells—how lack of diversity is hobbling business effectiveness and that improving inclusion will end up helping everyone without hurting any individual group.[12]

Of course, what constitutes the most persuasive business case will depend on the audience. The board might well be interested in financial data, and there's plenty of it. A 2015 McKinsey report on 366 public companies found that those in the top 25 percent for racial diversity among managers were 35 percent more likely to have financial returns above their industry mean; those in the top quartile for gender diversity in management were 15 percent more likely.[13] A 2013 study of 2,360 companies by a team at Credit Suisse found that companies with one or more women on the board reported higher average returns on equity, lower net debt-to-equity ratio, and better average growth. A 2012 study of the Standard & Poor's Composite 1500 that found that gender diversity increased the performance of companies focused on innovation. A 2009 study found that increases in racial diversity were associated with increased sales revenue, more customers, greater market share, and greater relative profits; increases in gender diversity were associated with increased sales, more customers, and greater profits.[14]

For managers, DEI needs to be tied to concrete managerial goals. Well-managed diverse teams enhance team performance. (See chapter 15 for more.) Why? Homogeneity makes us lazy, while diversity makes us smarter.[15]

Once you have your business case, remember Kotter, who notes that organizational change initiatives are often hobbled by "under-communicating the vision by a factor of 10."[16]

Step 3: Use metrics and accountability

Using metrics is another crucial element to treating diversity like a business problem. Just think of the axioms "we treasure what we measure" and "what gets measured gets done." If you aren't using metrics to establish baselines and measure progress, you're not serious about DEI, full stop.

A *Fortune* 250 fintech company sharply increased diversity by using metrics and accountability. It kept metrics on the candidates contacted, interviewed, and hired, and shared those metrics with the CEO, the hiring manager, and the relevant executive committee member. Equally important, achievement of diversity goals was linked to executive bonuses. After just eighteen months, 48 percent of newly hired executives at the VP level and above were white women or people of color, including 77 percent of newly hired SVPs.

Too often CEOs hire a CDO but then, when the person tries to develop key metrics, in-house lawyers get worried about legal risk and say no. CEOs need to send a strong message to in-house lawyers that the company is willing to shoulder some risk in order to implement effective DEI measures; a business goal for which you are unwilling to shoulder any risk is by definition not a serious business goal. (For more on keeping diversity metrics while controlling for legal risk, see our working paper on www .biasinterrupters.org.[17]) Or talk to any number of progressive Am Law 100 company-side senior attorneys who have deep experience, to assuage your general counsel that what we talk about in this book is not only doable but decreases legal risk overall.

Once again, Erby Foster at Clorox provides a road map for using two different kinds of metrics: outcome metrics and process metrics. Outcome metrics measure demographic groups' representation at different levels and parts of the company. Clorox made a commitment to outperform census data in the relevant geographical market in each of its eight functional divisions. Foster hired a company to provide a readout of census data, for example, of Black finance professionals in the Bay Area, using census data by job categories. This helped Clorox set targets (not quotas, which can give rise to legal problems).

Outcome metrics can tell you *whether* you have a problem, but not why or how to fix it. For that, you need process metrics, which provide a barrier analysis: what's going wrong, and where.

Foster's process metrics pinpointed three separate processes necessary to achieve the company's diversity goals, providing each unit with a hiring metric, a promotion metric, and a turnover metric. The hiring metric assessed both the diversity of the original pool of candidates and the hiring flow from each hiring manager, which enabled Foster to pinpoint *"Harry who only hires white guys."*

Another example of a process metric: relatively few minorities received high ratings at Clorox, which drove low rates of promotion and high rates of turnover. Still other process metrics begin from the data on how bias commonly plays out in workplace systems and then measure common patterns of bias (e.g., who gets mentions of personal style in performance evaluations). The most rigorous approach is to use the Workplace Experiences Survey to pinpoint whether bias exists, what business systems are affected, and how bias is affecting outcome measures like attrition and belonging. The alternative is to assume that common patterns of bias that affect most workplaces also affect yours.

The last crucial element is accountability. Foster classified each Clorox functional unit's progress in a simple dashboard as red, yellow, or green, and presented that information periodically to the C-suite. Note how this meets Kotter's rule of thumb: "If you can't communicate the vision to someone in five minutes or less," you lack an effective vision.[18]

Foster then went to the red and yellow units and assessed whether the problem was hiring, promotion, retention, or all three. If hiring stemmed from having a nondiverse original pool, Foster helped the unit develop a fix. For example, in sales the problem was that the department hired from only seven elite schools; Foster proposed adding a Black professional affinity group as the eighth core recruiting ground. He then flew the head of that affinity group to Clorox's

Oakland, California, headquarters to meet with the CEO, to jump-start a relationship that would allow the sourcing of top talent.

If Foster found that the problem was with promotion or turnover, he worked with the head of the functional unit to assess whether this was being driven by a few people or whether it was a broader problem, and then helped orchestrate a solution. Sometimes the focus was on external recruiting, but sometimes the focus was internal. For example, Clorox's finance department was 30 percent people of Asian descent, but, as Foster realized, many came from families where a career in sales was unthinkable. He hypothesized that meant that many Asians at Clorox not in sales roles were fascinated by sales but were culturally blocked from pursuing that path. So the sales division began promoting Asians from finance into roles that required analyzing sales data, and some then moved into working with customers.

Once Clorox began to treat diversity as a key business challenge, it made steady progress. Foster's goal was to create sustainable change; at one point, he protested that too many minorities were being hired too quickly: *"They got to like 62 percent, and I said, 'Oh, man, that's way too many, and I'm gonna tell you you're going to have big turnover in eighteen to twenty-four months because you can't absorb that much change in one given year.'"* He helped course-correct to a sustainable level of year-over-year change. Rome wasn't built in a day; over time Clorox sharply increased its diversity.

Foster stresses that it's important to pay attention to all levels of the company. The representation of minorities on the board increased from 10 percent to 40 percent; representation of women increased from 10 percent to 40 percent, too. Minorities in the C-suite increased from 10 percent to 25 percent; women in management increased from 34 percent to 43 percent; minority managers increased from 17 percent to 26 percent. Overall, minority representation increased from 28 percent to 31 percent.

Not surprisingly, once you apply standard business tools and treat diversity as a business problem, you can achieve your goals. No Clorox division head wanted to come up in the red zone; they all wanted to come up green. Foster's model tapped into another of Kotter's keys to culture change: the meetings at which division heads' metrics were shared with the CEO recognized and rewarded employees who nailed DEI goals, and made the inability to do so a bad career move. DEI goals were also part of the CEO and C-suite bonus formula.

Step 4: Debias HR systems

The next goal is to debias workplace systems. This is basically a job for HR, and it is detailed in chapter 14, so I will just give one example here. If your initial pool of job candidates lacks diversity, the first step is to reassess referral hiring if you do it. The second step is to do what Foster did at Clorox: develop a special recruitment program, which Kalev and Dobbin identify as a program of proven effectiveness with particularly strong positive impacts for African Americans, Asian Americans, Hispanics, and white women.[19]

Step 5: Change the incentives and capacity of middle management

"What gets rewarded gets done." This truism underlines another structural problem: no DEI initiative will be successful unless it changes incentives—something few CDOs can do today. That's why many DEI initiatives flounder when the CEO articulates ambitious goals and middle management ignores them.

At every organization a limited number of people are the key to changing the culture, notes James White, former CEO of Jamba Juice. He cites the example of one retail company where roughly 150 people control the work experience of the remaining one hundred thousand. Effective policies *enable* inclusion, but these middle managers hold the key to delivering it.

When White was at Jamba Juice, he instituted a new incentive system in which up to 20 percent of store managers' compensation was determined by engagement, climate, and organizational health scores. White used a variant of the Gallup Q^{12} survey; the Workplace Experiences Survey is another resource. Which measurement tool you use is less important than ensuring the tool assesses managerial effectiveness and impacts consequent compensation.

Step 6: Restructure access to opportunities

This final element of a CEO's DEI playbook is so important, and so complex, it deserves its own chapter: chapter 12. For now, let's just remember one thing:

Achieving DEI goals is leading change

At most companies, achieving DEI goals will entail a traditional change management process. The six-step protocol above accomplishes all eight of the steps outlined in John Kotter's famous model for leading change.[20] Building the business case creates a sense of urgency, and creates and communicates your vision. Empowering your DEI head and diversity committee creates a powerful coalition and helps people act on the vision. Using metrics creates visible short-term wins and ensures accountability. And changing the incentives for top brass and middle management removes obstacles to progress by holding people accountable for DEI goals, just as they are held accountable for other business goals.

Achieving results will not only improve measurable metrics; it will also make your company a much better place to work, and the word will spread. You will leave a legacy—not just that you helped to increase the share price from X to Y during your tenure, but that you helped the company change course and set itself up to create long-term success for all stakeholders.

How can a company change who gets access to opportunities? (Hint: Only the CEO can)

In industry after industry, we find that white men overwhelmingly feel they have fair access to desirable assignments (81 percent to 85 percent say so). Other groups, not so much. Women and professionals of color are eighteen to thirty-two percentage points less likely than white men to say their access to desirable assignments is fair; in architecture and engineering, only around half of Black women do (see figure 12-1).

Not only do white men report privileged access to career-enhancing work; they are sharply less likely to report unfair loads of less desirable work. Across industries, women report doing more administrative work than their colleagues at rates seventeen to twenty-two percentage points higher than white men (see figure 12-2). Multiracial women were most affected in architecture; women of Asian descent in engineering. Women of color in architecture are about twice

FIGURE 12-1

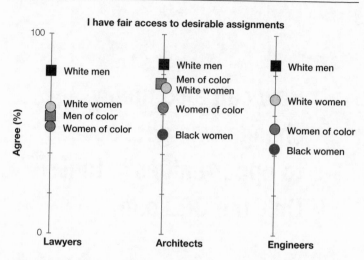

I have fair access to desirable assignments

Note: "Women of color" and "Men of color" include all people who identified as Black, Asian or Asian American, Latinx or Hispanic, multiracial, or any other nonwhite option. The data for the "of color" group provides an average of the data for each specific group. We did not receive enough responses from male engineers of color to draw conclusions.

Where available, the graphs highlight the group whose experiences diverge the most from white men's. When a single group is not highlighted, the percentage differentials between the individual groups were too small to be meaningful.

as likely as white men to report that they do more behind-the-scenes work than their colleagues; white women and men of color fell in between.

In other words, by the time performance evaluations come along, for many people the jig is up. They didn't get high-quality assignments, so they didn't develop the competencies, visibility, and networks they need to progress. I've seen time and again that unless a solution to this central and important problem starts with the CEO, it's nigh impossible to change the status quo: managers get caught

FIGURE 12-2

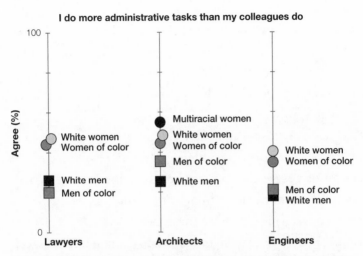

I do more administrative tasks than my colleagues do

Note: "Women of color" and "Men of color" include all people who identified as Black, Asian or Asian American (API), Latinx or Hispanic, multiracial, or any other nonwhite option. The data for the "of color" group provides an average of the data for each specific group. We did not receive enough responses from male engineers of color to draw conclusions.

Where available, the graphs highlight the group whose experiences diverge the most from white men's. When a single group is not highlighted, the percentage differentials between the individual groups were too small to be meaningful. However, for engineers, white women's experiences diverged the most from white men's on this statement.

up in the pressures of the day to day, and when projects come up, they have a vested interest in going back to the employee they trust.

Why should CEOs invest time in leading a solution? It's simple. It's not as if organizations have not *hired* women and people of color over the past thirty years. Often they have. The problem is that many organizations have hired people of color and women over and over again, only to have one after another leave, be replaced by someone else who also leaves, and on and on. Lack of opportunity plays an outsize role in creating this frustrating dynamic, in which companies spend more and more money on DEI but accomplish little.

Often we hear from managers that they keep going to the same few people with new work because those are the only people with the skill sets or the networks to get the job done. That's an admission that those managers are putting your company in a vulnerable position. If only a small circle of people have crucial firm-specific human capital, remember: they could walk out the door tomorrow. So it's good management to insist that managers develop a broader pool of talent. It may be in their short-term interest to keep going back to the same person, but it is not in the long-term interest of the company.

What constitutes desirable assignments differs from industry to industry. In architecture the glamour work is design work. *"I've seen younger women with architecture degrees pushed into more drafting, more into interiors and landscapes, while the men seem to think they are 'better' at designing the building structure and are given more face time with the clients."* In law, the glamour work is client contact and running closings or arguing in court. What's the office housework? *"We do the task list and manage the paralegals,"* one white woman reported. In investment banking, the glamour work is big deals—that's where the big money is; women often are seen as a good match for smaller clients.

Of course, everyone has to pay their dues. No one gets glamour work all the time, and junior people do more of the less glamorous work. That's life. The difference is that women often have more trouble getting rid of the less glamorous work than men do. In fact, senior women tell us over and over that they often end up doing lower-skill tasks— because the men they supervise refuse to do them! The solution is for management to send a clear message that this is a performance issue and will be treated as such.

At some companies, the conventional wisdom is that women keep the trains running because they're so much better at it. If that's true, typically it's because men know they can do it poorly and the only consequence will be that they are not asked to do it again, whereas women know that if they do it poorly, or refuse to do it, they will be seen as "prima donnas," "not a good team player," or simply inept. Exacerbating this dynamic at many small and not-so-small tech companies is the fact that women and people of color get handed diversity tasks—or even all the HR functions—to do on top of their regular jobs, but their performance evaluations assess only their performance at their official job.[1] Even women who don't mind doing the office housework need to work longer hours to succeed, because in order to get ahead, they have to find time to do the glamour work too.

While women of all races report larger loads of less-valued work, they also report less access to the glamour work. Men of color report less access, too. When consultancy GapJumpers analyzed the performance reviews of a tech company client, it found that women employees were 42 percent more likely than their male colleagues to be limited to lower-impact projects and that, as a result, far fewer women rose to senior roles.[2]

Equalizing access to opportunity is the toughest nut for a CEO to crack. CEOs don't personally hand out assignments to anyone but their direct reports. HR doesn't control assignments either: instead, they're handed out by tens or hundreds or thousands of managers. In-group favoritism means that this informality creates an invisible escalator for white men and an obstacle course for everyone else. Does this happen at your company? It's easy to find out whether there's fair access to opportunities. Just add the questions in the box to your next climate survey.

If you find you have a problem, two separate steps are needed to pin down the jellyfish of who gets access to

Does your company offer equal opportunity to all? Find out using these survey items. Ask people whether they agree with these statements:

- I have had the same access to desirable assignments as my colleagues.

- The level of work I am asked to perform is appropriate relative to my years of experience.

- Relative to my colleagues of comparable seniority, I am more likely to be assigned to high-profile tasks and teams.

opportunities. The hard step is to equalize access to the glamour work. The easier step is to fairly allocate the less-valued work.

Equalizing access to career-enhancing work

Access to opportunity typically requires access to both the right high-value assignments and the right high-value networks. The challenge for the CEO is that both typically come through informal processes. Two approaches can work, used either alone or together.

First, create *action learning teams.* The most direct approach to equalizing opportunity is to follow the path forged by James White.[3] When White joined Jamba Juice as CEO, he inherited a company in trouble and led a turnaround that stitched diversity deep into the corporate fabric. While increasing the market cap by 500 percent, he also increased diversity so much that, by the time he left, over 50 percent of the company's top two levels were women and people of color, and over 30 percent of the top three levels were.

White is African American; when he took over at Jamba Juice, management was 80 percent white men. By the end of his first year, so many women and people of color had been promoted that they made up half of managers. This rapid turnaround resulted from his appointment of action learning teams (ALTs) to accomplish business goals, including opening new distribution channels in airports and moving into global markets. His ALTs were cross-functional teams of fifteen to twenty people, with breakout groups of five to eight laser-focused to solve well-defined problems. Being appointed to an ALT was a high-profile assignment that was recognized as positioning employees for promotion. White purposely chose previously overlooked employees, which meant that these teams ended up being far more diverse than the company's workforce as a whole. So many employees got access to opportunity through ALTs that it spurred an abrupt increase in diversity at the top.

The ALTs were an essential reason White was able to grow both diversity and market cap simultaneously. Mandated to work on critical business initiatives, ALT members were given release time from their regular jobs and a ninety-day deadline. The theory behind action learning is that the people on the ground know best what's working well, and how to fix what's not. You just need to choose the right talent with the right mix of skills to solve a specific, well-defined business challenge. White has used this model scores of times at four different companies—Ralston Purina, Safeway, Gillette, and Jamba Juice. He finds that when you get the right mix of people, *"they always exceed your expectations."*

One potential pitfall: the assignments of the action learning teams must be company-critical assignments, not make-work. I have heard of ALTs set up as part of an out-of-the-package leadership program whose work ended up languishing on the vine. Serving on an ALT then becomes just another form of undervalued office housework.

Instead of, or in addition to, action learning teams, the CEO can assign a team to develop a system to equalize access to career-enhancing networks and plum assignments. With respect to plum assignments, the key is to pilot a more formal system. Choose some receptive and talented managers (or appoint an ALT) and task them with developing a typology of career-enhancing and less-valued work. Then launch a pilot in which another group of talented, receptive managers keep track of who gets the glamour work and who gets the less-valued work. (We have worksheets for meeting protocols, assignment typology, and manager assignments on www.biasinterrupters.org, as well as a survey to help you assess whether the office housework is fairly distributed.) Accountability matters: when managers know that higher-ups are keeping track of who gets the good work, this alone will help level the playing field.[4] If it turns out that's not enough, then the pilot will need to develop more formal mechanisms for allocating career-enhancing assignments.

Continue the pilot until you have a successful system. Then scale up.

Equalizing the load of less-valued work

Equalizing the load of less-valued work is far easier than equalizing career-enhancing assignments, but it's just as important. In industry after industry, women of all races report unequal loads of less-valued work at dramatically higher rates than men do. Methods for reallocating work that needs to get done but is not career-enhancing depend on the type of work involved.

Literal housework

In many offices, someone has to do things like cleaning up coffee cups and making sure there's water for a meeting. Across industries, we find it's women who mostly do it (see figure 12-3).

FIGURE 12-3

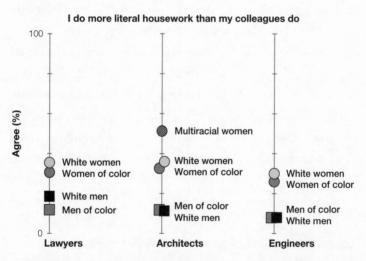

Note: "Women of color" and "Men of color" include all people who identified as Black, Asian or Asian American, Latinx or Hispanic, multiracial, or any other nonwhite option. The data for the "of color" group provides an average of the data for each specific group.

Where available, the graphs highlight the group whose experiences diverge the most from white men's. When a single group is not highlighted, the percentage differentials between the individual groups were too small to be meaningful. However, for engineers, white women's experiences diverged the most from white men's on this statement.

If you don't like what you find, then establish a formal system to rotate housework chores or make them part of the office manager's or admin's job. If your company celebrates birthdays and other occasions, there needs to be a sign-up system so that work is shared equally—and someone needs to monitor it to make sure that it's not only women signing up. When I ask large audiences who has planned an office party, typically about 70 percent of the women—and few if any men—raise their hands.

Administrative work

Women professionals typically report doing more administrative work than their colleagues at two to three times the rate that white men do.

There needs to be a formal system for deciding who takes the notes, fetches the documents needed during a meeting, handles logistics and scheduling, sends the follow-up email, consolidates everyone's comments. This is important, of course, because it's more difficult to participate in a meeting if you're in charge of taking notes, because handling logistics decreases time for more-valued work, and because allocating administrative work automatically to women sends a powerful message that women are expected to be worker bees, not leaders.

Two bias interrupters can work well here. The first is to rotate these tasks to everyone at a certain level. The second is the "plus one" system: invite a junior person to the meeting and have them take the notes—someone for whom this is a developmental opportunity because they otherwise would not be sitting in the room.

Diversity and other organizational development work

Alas, many companies say they value diversity work, mentoring, and community service work. But then they don't. *"I asked for a promotion and raise based on taking on a superior's role for a specific project. I was told that . . . many of these hours were dedicated to running the firm's volunteer projects—hence, not valuable to them, though they were heavily marketed—and that my salary was appropriate for someone at my level,"* said a white woman architect.

Two crucial lessons. First, don't say you value diversity work unless you actually do, both by providing the administrative and other support people need to do it effectively, and by treating it as mission-critical work that can lead to promotions, bonuses, and raises. Second, stop leaving diversity advocacy to the groups negatively affected by lack of diversity. It's easy to fix this problem, yet many companies never do.

Diversity advocacy is politically delicate, and often politically risky for every group except white men, so assigning it to groups that are already facing complicated office politics threatens to further undermine diversity.[5] Instead, if achieving DEI goals is truly a business goal, then appoint prominent people with sufficient political capital to achieve the goal and measure their success through objective metrics, on par with other metrics they need to meet. An obvious point that's often overlooked: if you appoint a diversity committee to overcome a particular bottleneck, it needs to include the gatekeeper who is creating the bottleneck. Otherwise, it's just ineffective make-work. For example, I heard from someone in charge of the committee to improve diversity in hiring that they had to submit hiring recommendations to the same supervisor who had created the problem—and who promptly rejected them.

Too often diversity is treated as undervalued office housework. This further jeopardizes the advancement of women and people of color, who have to spend a lot of time doing diversity work, which means they have to literally work more hours than white men if they want to get ahead. Again, the common practice of assigning women and people of color large loads of diversity advocacy threatens to undermine diversity, not enhance it.

Targeted sponsorship programs

People don't win opportunities all on their own. Sponsors help them. A sponsor is someone who is willing to use their position of influence and responsibility to advocate for a protégé and make tangible opportunities available. It's different from a mentor, who is more of a day-to-day confidant and supporter.

Research shows that men with broad entrepreneurial networks tend to get promoted early, but that women with similar networks typically get promoted early only if they also have a sponsor.[6]

In a study, Alexandra Kalev, Frank Dobbin, and Erin Kelly found that mentoring programs had positive effects for Asian American women, Latinas, Black women, Asian

American men, and Latinos (in that order).[7] The researchers did not separate sponsorship from mentorship, so some of the programs coded as mentoring programs probably involved sponsorship, while many no doubt did not. Networking programs were less effective, but did significantly help white women, Latinx people, and Asian Americans (in that order).

A forthcoming study of university mentorship/sponsorship programs found that the most effective target women and people of color specifically. The study found it was important to give sponsors a sense of ownership and autonomy, to encourage them to advocate for their protégés, and to pair sponsors and protégés from the same department.[8] Training that focused specifically on diversity tended to backfire.

As I have noted before, universities are different from companies. Professors expect extremely high levels of autonomy, whereas in the corporate context, managers are used to training and to having to get with the program. Still, we can adapt the findings to the corporate context, melding my work with a brilliant model from Laura Maechtlen at the law firm Seyfarth Shaw LLP. Mentoring programs that succeed have six elements:

1. **Defined goals.** The basic expectation should be that the sponsor and the protégé identify the protégé's desired next step in their career and the experiences they need in order to accomplish that. This will be crystallized in a sponsorship business plan, with goals and metrics. The sponsor's—and the protégé's—job

is to accomplish the business plan. Both sides should be evaluated on how effectively they pursue this goal. Obviously, sometimes life happens and goals are not met. But the guiding idea should be accountability. In most cases a good model is to have the protégé's defined goals include a short-term arc (often a year) and a long-term arc (often three to five years).

2. **Accountability.** In addition to accountability for achieving the goals articulated in the sponsorship business plan, the program should set up a regular schedule of check-ins to assure that the pair remains focused on making steady progress toward their goals.

3. **Selection of protégés.** Do an analysis of where diversity falls off, then target the group eligible for promotion to that level. Two alternatives exist for how to select protégés. One is to simply make this a targeted program for groups underrepresented in higher-level roles. The other is to make this a program open to anyone, but to accept people in inverse proportion to their group's representation in higher-level roles. I strongly recommend calling it a high-potential sponsorship program. Doing so will help overcome prove-it-again bias by christening participants as hi-po.

4. **Selection of sponsors.** Sponsors should be at a high enough level to enable them to help protégés achieve promotion to the next level. In some companies, sponsors can simply be told that successful sponsorship

is part of their jobs. In other companies where backlash against diversity is prevalent, it may be wiser to start off with senior sponsors who are either diversity champions or are at least open to the role, but still as senior in the organization as possible. Their incentives to accomplish this goal should be on par with their incentives for other goals.

5. **Training.** Training should be provided for both sponsors and protégés. The training for protégés should discuss issues like effective self-promotion, building an effective business network, and imposter syndrome. It should also help them identify the promotion they aspire to and think about the longer arc of their careers. Training for sponsors should involve talented, experienced sponsors sharing what has worked for them and what kinds of challenges their protégés commonly face. It should build in references to common forms of bias to equip them with strategies that work for members of different groups (which may be different from what works for white men).

6. **Start with a pilot.** If you are designing a program from scratch, it's a good idea to start with a small pilot and a group of people who are motivated to make it work. Build a prototype before you scale it; publicizing the concrete accomplishments the program achieved can help get the widespread buy-in you need to launch an effective scaled-up program.

Is this important enough for the CEO to dedicate time to?

Leveling the playing field with respect to opportunity is important because your company won't achieve its DEI goals unless you do. If bright and ambitious people feel blocked at your company, they will leave, regardless of race, gender, or any other category. And no one other than the CEO has the authority to put all the pieces in place to change access to opportunities. Managers, after all, control who gets access to plum assignments. They aren't likely to give up that control if the head of DEI or HR comes knocking; they just won't.

Leveling out who does the office housework is important too. Otherwise, women who are ambitious will need to do *both* the office housework that always seems to land on their doorstep *and* the career-enhancing work that gets them ahead. They will burn out. Then they will leave. Then you will hire more women, who will also leave.

CHAPTER 13

How can CDOs and HR get buy-in—and deliver— on DEI goals?

HR and CDOs will play the central role in ensuring sustainable companywide DEI progress. Organizational change can take a decade and, not to put too fine a point on it, CEOs come and go, but HR is eternal. The first key to sustainable progress on DEI is to build bias interrupters into organizational systems instead of relying on companywide conversations about inclusion. Inclusion conversations are no substitute for interrupting bias in your company's business systems, using metrics to establish baselines and measure progress.[*]

This chapter will provide concrete guidance on how to construct an evidence-based case for your company's DEI goals and the structural change needed to achieve them. There are three basic steps: gather data to build a case, design evidence-based interventions, and repeat.

---

[*]This section does not address employee resource groups (ERGs) and other measures that build community and capacity to help disadvantaged groups, because many excellent models exist for ERGs already.

Step 1: Gather metrics to determine if there is a problem

Even if you have buy-in at the top, it's important to collect metrics that assess whether you have a problem, how big it is, and where it shows up. No diversity effort can succeed without support from the middle, because it's midlevel managers who typically control access to opportunities.

Measuring demographic patterns in high-level jobs is important because they tell you whether your company has a problem getting women and people of color into leadership roles. But that is all they tell you. Such *outcome metrics* don't tell you why you have a problem or how to fix it. For that, you need *process metrics*.

It's easiest to explain process metrics in the context of hiring. To diagnose problems in hiring, you should be keeping track of who is in the original pool of applicants, who survives résumé review, who gets an interview, who survives the interviews, who gets offers, who accepts them, and (if salary is negotiable) what their starting salaries are. That's because the fix if you have a nondiverse applicant pool is totally different from the fix if no person of color makes it past the interview. Process metrics identify precisely what problem or problems you need to solve.

Another type of process metric provides a measurement of whether certain kinds of bias are playing out in a given system. For example, you can audit your performance evaluations to see if personal style—her "sharp elbows" or his "great smile"—gets equal airtime for different demographic groups. This will make it easy to see whether tightrope bias is affecting women and people of color. Studies suggest it usually is. (See chapter 4 for more on tightrope bias.)

One comprehensive approach is to use the Workplace Experiences Survey, which provides a complete picture of whether employees report experiencing bias, whether they feel various business systems are fair, and whether bias is affecting outcome measures such as belonging and intent to stay. The alternative is to collect the metrics needed for each business process to pinpoint whether bias is creeping in. Collecting the right metric can help CDOs and HR get the buy-in for an effective intervention.

For example, one creative HR employee at a professional services firm was trying to persuade her company to improve access to opportunities. So she did something simple. That firm already kept track of billable hours—and billable hours are the coin of the realm in professional services. She analyzed the hours in the two largest practice groups and found that, during the Covid-19 pandemic, white women were billing about one hundred fewer hours than white men, and people of color were billing two hundred to three hundred fewer hours. At her firm, professionals who did not bill enough hours did not thrive, so her findings were persuasive to leadership.

Another example comes from a company with a problem I call "magic jumpers." That's when white men jump up a level (or two) in a company where this rarely or never happens to women and people of color. It's very common.

Count the number of magic jumpers and keep track of who they are. A simple demographic breakdown can be telling—and persuasive.

Metrics are also important for other reasons. They are crucial for establishing baselines and measuring whether what you are doing is effective. They can help you celebrate small wins that build support for DEI efforts. Finally, given that eliminating bias is not a one-and-done proposition, they can keep guiding you toward your goal.

You may get pushback from in-house lawyers worried that keeping metrics will result in legal risk. If you do, refer them to the white paper, *Keeping Diversity Metrics While Controlling for Legal Risk* at www.biasinterrupters.org. You can also introduce your legal department to some progressive outside counsel who have deep experience in keeping clients safe while they implement bold DEI initiatives. If your legal team's go-to outside counsel is more conservative, perhaps you could use a second opinion.

Keep in mind that businesses are willing to shoulder some level of legal risk for any business initiative they truly care about, so if your company insists on "zero risk tolerance" in the DEI context, that's an eloquent way to say that diversity is not really a priority for the company. The risks can be reasonably mitigated by following the protocol described in the white paper mentioned above. But the key point is that the risk of negative publicity, lawsuits, and employee turnover from doing nothing, or too little, on DEI far outweigh the risks of collecting some data.

Step 2: Use evidence-based tool kits

Small steps can produce big change—if they are evidence-based steps. Throughout this book, we've discussed several ways that small interventions created a more-level playing field. Here's where you take the data you gathered in Step 1 and try different interventions to interrupt the bias you've documented. Which interventions change the data?

While this step does involve a lot of experimenting, it's important to emphasize that you're not just throwing stuff at the wall to see what sticks; you can use the social science described in this book to build a structured, strategic initiative. In Chapter 14, I describe in more detail how to interrupt bias in hiring and performance evaluations so you can get a concrete sense of the approach to those crucial business systems.

Step 3: Keep at it

You will not eliminate all the bias at your company with a single effort or in a single year—and that should not be the goal. The goal should be to take small steps consistently. If you build these kinds of evidence-based tweaks into your fundamental business systems, the organizational change you effect will be more resilient and long-lasting than a CEO-driven, conversation-based culture change. Use metrics to measure progress, and go methodically—implementing evidence-based change after evidence-based change, deep in the day-to-day systems, and educating managers at all levels.

Instead of trying to boil the ocean—and I know you know this—go for small wins at first to build up support for sustained organizational change.[1] Do a pilot with some receptive managers, and use your successes to pave the way for future steps.

The 1 Percent Solution

If you are an experienced HR or DEI professional, you know how many stakeholders there are in determining who gets hired at your organization, who gets access to valued opportunities, who gets a promotion, and who gets a raise. You know only too well that adjusting any of the above will involve a complex organizational change process. And you know, only too well, how persistent and creative you need to be to effect organizational change. My advice: relentless pursuit of the 1 percent. Keep improving organizational systems in ways that are politically feasible right now, and then widely publicize the fruits of your labors to build political support for steps that will lead to other 1 percent improvements. I've worked with a lot of talented people in HR and DEI. I know how impossible what I'm asking you to do is. And I know you can do it.

CHAPTER 14

How can HR and DEI departments work together to interrupt bias in basic business systems?

Be warned, this chapter gets geeky. This book's central message is that DEI goals are best treated as technical problems that require detailed, evidenced-based solutions. Achieving consistent 1 percent gains often will not require much more than tweaks to business systems, if the organization has mature HR systems. But there are quite a lot of tweaks. If that's your jam, read on!

Some of what's here has been said in earlier chapters, but I included it again because it will be convenient to have it all in one place.

Bias interrupters tool kit for recruiting and hiring

In 2015, only 10 percent of new data scientists at Airbnb were women. By implementing the kind of best practices described below, the company increased female new hires to

47 percent in just one year, doubling its overall number of female data scientists, from 15 percent to 30 percent.

The first step was to use data analysis to find out that 30 percent of its data scientist applicants were women. Second, the company increased conversion (the proportion of applicants hired) by taking some steps to interrupt bias in résumé review, such as providing a detailed description of what to look for and making ratings clearer and more objective. (It also experimented with removing candidates' names from résumés, an experiment it later abandoned.) Third, Airbnb changed the interviewing process to avoid the situation where women candidates face unending rooms of male-only interviewers, requiring instead that women make up at least half of interview panels for female candidates. It also offered all candidates—men as well as women—an informal coffee chat with a member of the interview panel so they would not face a room full of unfamiliar faces; this is yet another example of how improving business processes helps every group. In assessing interviews, Airbnb focused the discussions about the candidates on the objective traits of the presentation rather than the subjective interpretations of the interviewers. Finally, it created "Small Talks, Big Data"—a series of public data science talks given by a panel of women from diverse racial and ethnic backgrounds. Along with accompanying blog posts by women at the company, this sent the message that Airbnb was a good place for women to work in data science.[1]

Your company, too, can use bias interrupters to improve diversity in hiring in short order.

Hiring is not one process; it's several, sometimes divided into two separate departments: recruiting and HR. Typically, individual managers are involved too. Train everyone involved in the hiring process to spot and interrupt bias. Empower them to offer solutions that would interrupt it. And consider having HR professionals or team members get additional, in-depth, social science–backed training to better guide the hiring process. (We have a worksheet on identifying and interrupting bias in hiring on www .biasinterrupters.org, which summarizes in two pages some forty years of research on bias based on race, gender, and social class.)

Getting everyone involved is important because hiring more women and people of color means making tweaks to the typical hiring process at *every* stage of the hiring process, from the initial job posting to the offer letter.

Assemble a diverse pool and write the job ad

It will be exceedingly difficult to hire more women and minorities if your pool of candidates is overwhelmingly white and male. There are several ways to ensure a more diverse set of applicants.

Insist that the pool of candidates contain multiple women and people of color

Creating a diverse pool is the single most important step to interrupt bias—and it doesn't mean adding one diversity candidate. The odds of hiring a woman are seventy-nine times greater if there are at least two women in the finalist pool; the odds of hiring a person of color are 194 times greater.[2] I have heard persistent reports that in tech companies the requirement for a diverse pool is not accompanied by metrics measuring who is actually chosen for the job. That tick-the-box approach isn't going to change anything.

Monitor referral hiring

If your company relies on referral hiring, keep track of that stream of candidates to see whether it lacks diversity. If it does, open up a discussion about whether to eliminate referral hiring or balance it out with targeted outreach programming to other groups.

Use targeted recruitment

Targeted recruitment of women or people of color has positive effects for every group, with the strongest effect for Black professionals, Asian Americans, and white women.[3] The standard is to recruit more heavily at historically black colleges and universities (HBCUs); other important resources are job fairs, affinity networks, conferences, and training programs aimed at women, LGBTQ+ people, or people of color in relevant fields. For more senior roles, the best approach may be to use a specialist in diversity recruiting. In addition to these steps, consider creative uses of LinkedIn to help reach out to a diverse range of candidates.

Consider candidates from multitiered schools and/or use skills-based screening

Latinx professionals are more likely to seek higher education opportunities closer to where they grew up, so it is important, both for them and for first-gen professionals of all races, not to recruit only from networks of elite institutions. As discussed in chapter 5, top students from lower-ranked schools are often as successful as those from top-ranked schools—and easier to retain.[4] If you're in tech, a company like GapJumpers can help you recruit for technical positions by using skills tests rather than degrees.

Highlight existing employees to attract others

If the candidates you want are not applying for your jobs, get the word out that your company is a great place to work for women and people of color. For example, you might follow Airbnb's example of offering public talks and blog posts by women to show the company is a good destination for female data scientists.

Change the wording of your job postings

Using words associated with masculine stereotypes in job ads, like "aggressive," can depress the number of female applicants, who may not feel they would be a good fit for your culture. (See chapters 4 and 6 for more background on why.) Avoid those words and instead, use words like "responsible" and "conscientious"; studies suggest more women will respond to ads like this, and the number of men who apply won't drop—it may even rise. Separate analyses by LinkedIn

De-gender Job Postings

Here are some masculine words commonly used in job postings that tend to decrease the number of women applicants: determined, autonomous, outstanding, direct, active, analytical, rational, push, outspoken, corporate influence, assert.

To increase women applicants, use feminine words: committed, responsible, talents, responsible for employees, sociable, conscientious, sensible, sincere, support, cooperate, social responsibility, honest, communicate.

and ZipRecruiter have found that gender-neutral job postings were more appealing to both men and women and resulted in more applications overall.[5] Again, creating a fairer playing field helps everyone.

Explicitly stating in the job ad that salary is negotiable can equalize the proportions of men and women who negotiate their salaries—which can reduce a gender gap in pay.[6] As discussed in chapter 4, many women are reluctant to negotiate for fear of not being perceived as suitably "modest, self-effacing, and nice."[7]

Upgrade résumé reviews

Before a résumé review begins, hold a meeting to go over how to identify and interrupt bias in hiring (there's one at www.biasinterrupters.org). An experiment showed that it is important to review this information orally, rather than just giving people a worksheet. Here are some other steps that can help:

Precommit to what's important—and require accountability

Put in writing what qualifications are important, both in entry-level and in lateral hiring. When qualifications are waived for a specific candidate, require an explanation of why—and keep track of which candidates receive these waivers.

Rate independently, use a consistent rating scale, and discount outliers

Establish clear grading rubrics and ensure that everyone grades on the same scale. When a group of people are evaluating candidates, the best procedure is for each evaluator to give their rating independently, without consultation. Consider having each résumé reviewed by two or more managers and averaging the score.[8] If possible, discount outliers—reviewers who disproportionately loved or loathed a candidate.

Ask questions about résumé gaps

Don't count gaps in a résumé as an automatic negative. Instead, give the candidate an opportunity to explain their work history and anything that might seem unusual about it.[9] There are many, many reasons people might have a gap between jobs. Judge them by the work they've done, not the time they've missed. This is fairer to people with family caregiving responsibilities, as well as anyone who has had to take time off from work for serious health issues like cancer. If someone has taken time away from paid work to look after children or aging parents, don't infer that they'll be less committed to the job they're applying for now.

Improve interviews

Until now, the hiring process has been rather one-sided: the candidates sent in their applications and awaited your judgment. Now, the balance of power has started to shift. During the job interview, the candidate still obviously wants to make a good impression, but they are also judging the people they meet just as much as they're being judged. This is your organization's chance to make a good impression. To make sure you come across well, take a couple of steps:

Provide all candidates with a handout detailing expectations

This can level the playing field for first-gen professionals, Asian Americans, women, and introverts; these are all groups more likely to feel pressure to be modest or self-effacing. Setting expectations clearly allows them to make their best case for themselves. One handout we've used includes advice like, "Present yourself with quiet confidence. Bluster doesn't work well here, nor does excessive modesty." We also think it's a good idea to remind candidates of the qualities and skills you're looking for and share the metrics you'll use to interviewees after the conversation.

Use structured interviews and ratings

Ask every candidate the same list of questions. Ask questions directly relevant to the job.[10] Don't ask about hobbies and the like unless your goal is to replicate your existing workforce.

After the interview is over, interviewers should rate the candidate using a consistent rating scale. After collecting these ratings, discount the outliers—the interviewers who either ranted or raved about the candidate—as you did with the résumé screening process.

Rethink culture fit

If culture fit is used in hiring, first ask the hiring manager to articulate in writing what "culture fit" means. Then keep track of who is seen as a poor fit and look for demographic patterns. This isn't only about people of color and white women; keep track of first-gen candidates as well. If the culture fit criterion is having an exclusionary effect, the company needs to define culture fit in terms of work-relevant skills and dispositions, not in terms of preferred leisure activities or the lunch test (would I like to have lunch with this person?). (See chapter 6 for more on what "fit" means.) Another problem with the concept of culture fit is that, once "fit" is felt, disqualifying factors and attributes may well be minimized or ignored, and objective requirements that have been applied to others may be set aside.

Ask performance-based questions and/or use work sample screenings

Questions like "Tell me about a time you had too many things to do and had to prioritize" provide concrete information about job-relevant skills.[11] If applicable, ask candidates to take a skills-based assessment. For example, if part of the job is analyzing data sets and making recommendations, ask the candidate to do that. If part of the job involves writing, ask candidates to submit writing samples.

Track what happens after the interview

If women, people of color, and first-gen white men are getting called in for interviews but not being offered jobs at the end of the process, conduct an audit of your interview process. Are these candidates rated differently by interviewers? Are interviewers treating them differently than in-group candidates? A study of economists found that, when presenting research to peers, women get more questions than men, including more questions that are patronizing, disruptive, demeaning, or hostile.[12] The same study showed that women were interrupted more frequently. If your company is attracting a diverse pool of applicants, but those people are not making it through the interview process, it's fair to ask if dynamics like these could be at play.

Bias interrupters tool kit for performance evaluations

Interrupting bias in performance evaluations is a lot more straightforward.

- **Appoint and train people to interrupt bias.** Train HR professionals or senior managers to spot the types of bias we've been discussing in this book. Our research again shows that formal training, where these issues are discussed aloud, is more impactful than just hand-ing out worksheets: when we asked HR people to read one of the performance evaluation worksheets on www.biasinterrupters.org aloud, it resulted in better performance evaluations and higher bonuses for Black men, Black women, and white women. Have trained bias interrupters read performance evaluations before they become final. If the evaluations of a given su-pervisor show consistent patterns of bias, the trained bias interrupter should intervene. Without making a heavy-handed judgment, they can present some of the data discussed in this book and ask the supervisor to take another look at their evaluations.

- **Redesign the evaluation form.** First, provide clear and specific performance criteria, and ask for evidence from the rating period that justifies any numerical rat-ing. This approach is powerful. (See chapter 7.) Sec-ond, separate out performance and potential. This is important because white men, but not other groups, tend to be judged on potential and given the benefit of the doubt. (See chapter 3.) Third, separately assess personal style issues that need to be addressed and skill sets that need to be developed. This will make it easy to spot if women and people of color are faulted for issues of personal style that white men get a pass for. (See chapter 4.)

- **Provide guidelines if self-evaluations are part of your process.** Giving guidance for self-evaluations helps

ensure that everyone knows how to promote themselves effectively and sends the message they are
expected to do so. For example, make it clear that
everyone is expected to provide examples of work
they're especially proud of. Ask everyone to give an
example of an area where they could improve. (For
more, see chapter 5.)

- **Have the people you've trained to be bias interrupters play
an active role in calibration meetings and use rubrics.** If
calibration meetings involve unstructured horse-
trading, that's a petri dish for bias, as are forced rankings. Abandon them, or at least provide a rubric so
that everyone is judged objectively and in writing on
the same criteria—and then look for demographic
patterns. Pay close attention to whether objective requirements are waived for some groups more
than others.

- **Don't eliminate your performance appraisal system!**
Women and people of color already get less feedback,
and less honest feedback. Offering feedback on the
fly will exacerbate the problem: an experiment found
that women were told "gendered white lies"—people
avoided telling them hard truths.[13] Our data suggests
this effect may be widespread, and particularly strong
for Black women; in architecture, they are more than
three times as likely as white men to report getting
less honest feedback than their colleagues. And it's not
just architecture: in law, only about a fifth of white

men, but 40 percent of men of color, report they don't receive constructive feedback.[14] (More about this in chapter 15.)

HR should work closely with DEI

There are probably few surprises here. Since this chapter is designed chiefly for HR professionals, I probably haven't told you much you didn't already know. But by writing it all down, with data, I hope I have made it easier for you to get the time, resources, and buy-in to implement many of the changes I suspect were already on your wish list.

CHAPTER 15

How can individual managers help move the needle—and manage more effectively?

This chapter provides you with fifteen concrete steps any manager can take to become an inclusive leader, even if you don't run the organization. The lesson is worth learning: well-managed diverse teams outperform homogeneous ones, are more committed, and are better at making decisions and solving problems.[1] Here are two reasons why:

- **Gender-diverse teams are higher in collective intelligence.** The group's collective intelligence is more than twice as important as individual team members' intelligence in determining team performance, and is more important in influencing team satisfaction, cohesion, and motivation. Collective intelligence is how well the team works together. What determines it? More communication, even distribution of speaking turns, and being able to "read the mind in the eyes."

Women tend to be strong on all three, which is why gender-balanced teams tend to have higher collective intelligence than male-only teams.[2]

- **Racially diverse teams avoid groupthink and work harder.** One study found racially diverse groups were better at considering the facts; they also made fewer errors in recalling relevant information.[3] Another found that racial diversity led to broader thinking and consideration of alternatives than homogeneous teams.[4]

Don't have overconfidence in confidence: homogeneous teams are surer of their answers despite the fact that diverse groups perform better, according to findings by psychologist Katherine Phillips and her coauthors.[5]

One reason it's so important for managers to play an active role is that advocating for diversity can be costly—except if they are white men.[6] This chapter will focus on four arenas over which individual managers have a lot of control: work assignments, meetings, work-life balance, and feedback (including how to respond to racist or sexist comments in the moment). Some of the material in this chapter appears in prior chapters, but I suspect it will be useful to have it all in one place.

Equalize access to opportunity

Evening out access to opportunity entails two separate tasks. First, you have to even out who does the office housework: administrative tasks, keeping-the-trains-running work, even party planning. Then you have to even out access to the glamour work that leads to promotion. This is explained in more detail in chapter 12; it's summarized here for simplicity.

Set up a rotation for office housework—don't ask for volunteers

"I always give these tasks to women because they do them well" or "because they volunteer" are common refrains. They typically reflect an environment where men suffer few consequences for bypassing or doing a poor job on low-value work, while women who do the same are seen as prima donnas or incompetent. Particularly when administrative staff is limited, a rotation helps level out the playing field and makes it clear that everyone is expected to contribute to the more routine tasks, from cleaning up after an event to sending the post-meeting follow-up email. Don't staff these tasks by asking for volunteers or by just leaving it to someone to step up. If you do, women will feel under powerful pressure to volunteer, while men will feel free not to.

Keep track of who is getting high-profile opportunities

If you don't keep track of who gets valued projects, bias may be choking off opportunity for some groups. Identify the career-advancing assignments and networking opportunities in your department. Spend the next month keeping track of who has access to these chances. If you find a problem, fix it.

Sometimes we hear, "I keep giving plum assignments to a small group—but they're the only ones with the skills to do them!" If you only have a small circle capable of handling a highly valued task, widen that circle. It might take more time in the short run, but you'll be glad you invested that time when somebody you relied on leaves the company or transfers to a new team. Otherwise, as a (literal) rocket scientist explained, *"You have a single-point system failure if someone decides to retire."*

Another approach is to use the "plus one" system. Assign a more junior person to shadow a senior one to develop new skills—and make sure they take notes.

Reward lower-profile contributions

If certain low-profile tasks are important, reward them. If they aren't important, eliminate them. Be honest. Don't say you deeply value mentoring but then discount its importance when someone does it well. The same applies to diversity work, and running the internship program, and countless other vital but unglamorous tasks. Integrating these and other lower-profile contributions into individual goal setting, and then evaluating them during performance reviews, is a good start.

"You've got to pay your dues." True, but often white men transition seamlessly out of low-profile work while others find it difficult or impossible to do so. Even when white women and people of color win exciting new assignments, they're often expected to keep doing the scut work they did earlier in their careers.

The key management point is that most lower-profile work can be a developmental opportunity if assigned to someone at the correct level. It may be convenient to have someone continue to do something you know they're good at—but if it's a drag on the person's advancement, they'll leave. Think long term.

Run inclusive meetings

Bias plays out in meetings in ways that can be downright dangerous for your company. Remember: men with expertise are *more* influential than men without it, while women with expertise are *less* influential than women without it. As a result, groups with a female expert perform less well than groups with male experts (who were actually listened to!).[7] In meetings that include more men than women, women typically participate about 25 percent less than men do.[8] Men also interrupt women much more than vice versa.[9] In engineering and architecture, about half of women of all races, but only about one-sixth of white men, say they are interrupted more than their colleagues.

Racial stereotypes affect meeting dynamics in several ways. For example, the percentage of men of color who report being interrupted more than their colleagues is twice as high as the percentage of white men who do. And a Black tech executive told me about a meeting during which she said little, while the only other woman, an Asian American, contributed a lot. But she later heard that people thought she had "dominated" the conversation while her colleague had been "very quiet."

Interrupt excessive interruptions

Notice whether men are consistently interrupting women. If they are, a calm, authoritative "Let's let her finish" should send the message to most. If more is needed, take someone aside and tell them that you appreciate their fervor but they need to wait their turn.

Call out the stolen idea

If someone takes credit for an idea a colleague originally offered, say, "Yes, I agree: I liked Sandra's point too." If the person doesn't get the message, talk to them privately later and tell them to cut it out.

Help out introverts and anyone with a modesty mandate

If people don't offer their opinions freely, give them a heads-up that you plan to call on them. That will give a little push to women, Asian Americans, first-gen professionals, and anyone who's introverted or shy. It's particularly important to invite women experts to speak up. Sending the meeting agenda around in advance can help everyone— especially quieter team members—prepare.

Remember, it's a business meeting

Business meetings should take place in the office, not on the golf course, a university club, or your favorite concert venue. Otherwise, you're giving an artificial advantage to people whose personal interests overlap with yours. If you do schedule meetings around your interests (e.g., a walking meeting), be proactive in ensuring that those who don't share them get equal opportunities.

Be respectful of people's nonwork commitments

Keep in mind that only 12 percent of college-educated women work over fifty hours a week—and that many men feel they need to be involved with children's daily care to be a good father.[10] Work-life balance is the second most valued workplace benefit by millennials.[11] (What's the first? Training and development.) To learn more, read chapter 9.

Obviously, the work needs to get done, but you will have a more stable and committed team if you respect people's nonwork commitments. Remember, most employees are in two-career couples, and they may have established routines that require them to pick up the kids or relieve elders' care-givers at the beginning or end of the day. Others have "furry children" who need a walk (aka pets).

Schedule meetings during business hours

Wherever possible, schedule meetings during normal working hours. Otherwise, you risk creating bias against caregivers. Not everyone can stick around for a 6 p.m. discussion.

Allow remote work if your company permits you to

Eighty-three percent of employers say that remote work went well during the Covid-19 pandemic.[12] Allow people to work from home a few days a week and keep a schedule that works for them. Many employees who need to be home at a specific time are happy to finish their tasks after the kids are in bed.

Don't make assumptions

Last but not least, don't assume that a mother doesn't want a career-enhancing assignment because it will involve travel or be time-consuming. Ask her, making it clear that if she says no now, you will keep her in mind for other opportunities in the future—then do so. Heads up: you should do this for fathers, too. As you know, treating women differently than men can spell trouble.

Give effective feedback (including about racist or sexist comments)

High-performing teams receive positive and negative feedback at roughly a 6:1 ratio, which means that if your team is human and makes mistakes, you need to provide lots of positive feedback in order to make room for the negative feedback.[13] A simple "feedback sandwich," with positive on either end and negative in the middle, isn't enough. People can handle negative feedback if it is objective and delivered with the intent to help someone improve, rather than to beat someone down.

You need a system

Giving feedback needs to become a habit. Research shows that the best way to develop a new habit is to set aside time to do it and to keep your initial goals modest.[14] Build a system to ensure everyone gets equal amounts of feedback, and keep track of whom you give it to so that no one is left out.

Give feedback to everyone

Women and people of color tend to get less specific, and less honest, feedback—which means they aren't always given a chance to improve their performance.[15] *"I don't think he gave me honest feedback . . . I think he meant well, and he just didn't want to offend me, but sometimes it had the opposite effect and made me feel undermanaged,"* said a woman engineer. One experiment had participants assess essays without knowing the sex of the writer, then randomly told them the essay was written by either a man or a woman. Subjects who thought the writer was a woman tended to tell "little white lies" that inflated their earlier assessment.[16]

Discuss common biases before you write performance evaluations

We were somewhat surprised to find that a simple experiment, taking less than five minutes, resulted in fairer reviews—and higher bonuses—for Black men and women and white women. We asked people to read aloud a two-page worksheet on interrupting bias in performance evaluations. Interestingly, reading it aloud was much more effective than asking people to read the material silently. Given the strength of the effects we found, I suggest you take the time to read and discuss common biases with those you supervise who evaluate others. You can find it, and several worksheets for managers, at www.biasinterrupters.org.

Level the playing field with respect to self-promotion

Asian Americans, first-generation professionals, and women are often raised with a modesty mandate—and may encounter more pushback for self-promotion than white men, which makes them even more reluctant to advocate for themselves.[17] Giving clear guidance on what you'd like to see in a self-appraisal ensures that everyone knows how to promote themselves effectively and sends the message that they are expected to do so. Also, if you rely heavily on self-promotion to learn about your reports' accomplishments, consider setting up a more formal system for doing so. Some people send out an email once a month to celebrate the successes of their team; that encourages modest people to share as well.

Be matter-of-fact and firm

Wow, someone just said the most racist or sexist thing you've ever heard. Remember: you're the leader—you are modeling for your team what is appropriate and what isn't. Drama isn't needed, but firmness is. "Kim, that was a very inappropriate comment, and not aligned with who we are as a company" is all you need to say in public. Talk to Kim in private and make sure they understand why the comment was inappropriate. Then talk to anyone who heard the comment and might have been upset by it. Say, "I want to reiterate that I found Kim's comment inappropriate, and that I have talked with Kim to say we do not expect that kind of thing in the future. But I also wanted to give you the opportunity to have a direct conversation with me, so that I can make sure I am doing what I need to do to run an inclusive team in which we all feel we can do our best work." If the person says, "No, I'm OK," then respect that—no need to put them on the spot. But reiterate that you have an open door should they need to discuss this, or anything else, in the future.

For more on giving feedback, I recommend a short guide by Sloan R. Weitzel, *Feedback That Works: How to Build and Deliver Your Message.*

You don't have to be perfect

You don't have to be perfect to be a good manager. If you do these fifteen things, or even some of them, with sincerity, that will go a long way toward creating the goodwill you'll need when you make mistakes. In addition, you'll be running a team where everyone can give you their best work. That means you'll be a better manager. And a better human being, too. We can all use that.

Conclusion

Achieving both diversity and inclusion can be done with the tools we have forged over more than a century to achieve any business goal: data, metrics, and persistence.

I won't say it's always easy, but then nothing worth doing ever is. I will say it's doable, and that many have already taken important steps. I'm excited to share your journey, so if you try the approach laid out in this book—or anything else that really works—please let us revel in your success. Send us a note at www.biasinterrupters.org. We look forward to hearing from you.

Don't get discouraged if your company struggles on its path to success. Social inequality is frustratingly resilient, but change isn't impossible. When I was young(ish) in the 1980s, anti-gay bias was extraordinarily open and virulent. My memories of that time stretch from the AIDS crisis of the 1980s to the brutal murder of Matthew Shepard in 1998. In the 1990s, "Don't Ask, Don't Tell" and the Defense of Marriage Act were the law of the land.

But things have changed. Remember how hard it is to change implicit bias—the rate at which negative stereotypes are triggered in your brain? Well, implicit anti-gay bias fell by 33 percentage points between 1988 and 2016.[1] And between 2004 and 2015, same-sex marriage went from being illegal across the United States to being recognized in all 50 states. That's truly extraordinary. What fueled these changes was most likely the message that many gay people want what most straight people want: to build a family with someone they love.

I hope this book will show leaders at all levels that people of color, women, and first-gen professionals also just want what white men from college-educated families want: a workplace where they feel they can get a fair shake. Everyone wants a world where, if they work hard, they can get ahead to the best of their abilities. When we achieve that together—for everyone—everyone wins. Companies will be tapping the full talent pool. Individuals will be able to do their best work. The world will be a better, fairer place. That's where we're headed, folks. Join me.

Methodology

The research on workplace bias described in this book comes from data collected using the Workplace Experiences Survey. The WES is a ten-minute survey designed to examine how bias based on gender, race/ethnicity, and social class plays out in everyday interactions in the workplace. Participants in each survey sample were asked to fill out quantitative questions in the WES while thinking about their current or most recent workplace, and also had the opportunity to write qualitative comments that are shared throughout this book.

Across fourteen different studies, approximately 18,000 participants have taken the WES. This includes nationwide studies of STEM professors and professionals, lawyers, engineers, architectural professionals, cross-industry professionals, and individuals at private organizations. These surveys are not nationally representative, although they do include individuals from across the United States as well as engineers in India. Due to the small number of men of color in our study of engineers, we do not report those results.

The WES seeks to ask about race/ethnicity in the most inclusive way, which has evolved over time. Therefore, some of the surveys discussed in this book use the term "Asian Americans" and some use "people of Asian descent" (which includes immigrants).

Quantitative WES data was collected using a 1–6 Likert scale: strongly disagree to strongly agree. Analyses examining differences in the experiences of different groups were conducted using one-way ANOVAs and regression analyses. Data is presented in the form of percentages of agreement for readers' ease of understanding: 1–3 (strongly disagree to slightly disagree) is considered a response of "no" and 4–6 (slightly agree to strongly agree) is considered a response of "yes."

NOTES

Chapter 1

1. Stephen J. Dubner, "How to Fix the Hot Mess of U.S. Healthcare," March 31, 2021, in *Freakonomics*, produced by Zack Lapinski, podcast, https://freakonomics.com/podcast/healthcare-costs.

2. Evan Hill et al., "How George Floyd Was Killed in Police Custody," *New York Times*, May 31, 2020, https://www.nytimes.com/2020/05/31/us/george-floyd-investigation.html.

3. Alexandra Kalev, Frank Dobbin, and Erin Kelly, "Best Practices or Best Guesses? Assessing the Efficacy of Corporate Affirmative Action and Diversity Policies," *American Sociological Review* 71, no. 4 (2006): 589–617.

4. Christopher Chabris and Daniel Simons, "The Invisible Gorilla," accessed April 30, 2021, http://theinvisiblegorilla.com/gorilla_experiment.html.

5. Marianne Bertrand and Sendhil Mullainathan, "Are Emily and Greg More Employable Than Lakisha and Jamal? A Field Experiment on Labor Market Discrimination," *American Economic Review* 94, no. 4 (2004): 991–1013.

6. Shelley J. Correll, Stephen Benard, and In Paik, "Getting a Job: Is there a Motherhood Penalty?" *American Journal of Sociology* 112, no. 5 (2007): 1297–1339.

7. Joan C. Williams and Rachel Dempsey, *What Works for Women at Work* (New York: New York University Press, 2014).

8. Joan C. Williams et al., "Walking the Tightrope: An Examination of Bias in India's Engineering Workplace," Society of Women Engineers and the Center for WorkLife Law, 2018, https://worklifelaw.org/wp-content/uploads/2018/10/Walking-the-Tightrope-Bias-Indias-Engineering-Workplace.pdf; Joan C. Williams et al., "Climate Control: Gender and Racial Bias in Engineering?" Society of Women Engineers and the Center for WorkLife Law, 2016, https://worklifelaw.org/publications/Climate-Control-Gender-And-Racial-Bias-In-Engineering.pdf; Joan C. Williams, Katherine W. Phillips, and

Erika V. Hall, "Double Jeopardy? Gender Bias Against Women of Color in Science," The Center for WorkLife Law, 2015, https://worklifelaw .org/publications/Double-Jeopardy-Report_v6_full_web-sm.pdf; Joan C. Williams et al., "You Can't Change What You Can't See: Interrupting Racial and Gender Bias in the Legal Profession," American Bar Association and Minority Corporate Counsel Association, 2018; Joan C. Williams, Rachel Korn, and Rachel Maas, "The Elephant in the (Well-Designed) Room: An Investigation into Bias in the Architecture Profession," The Center for WorkLife Law, forthcoming 2021; Joan C. Williams, Rachel Korn, and Rachel Maas, "Pinning Down the Jellyfish: Women of Color in Tech," The Center for WorkLife Law, forthcoming 2021.

9. Joan C. Williams et al., "Climate Control."

10. Joan C. Williams et al., "You Can't Change What You Can't See."

11. Joan C. Williams et al., "Climate Control."

12. Joan C. Williams et al., "You Can't Change What You Can't See."

13. Iris Bohnet, "What Works: Gender Equality by Design," *Diplomatic Courier* 12, no. 2 (February 2018): 32–33.

14. Aparna Joshi, Jooyeon Son, and Hyuntak Roh, "When Can Women Close the Gap? A Meta-Analytic Test of Sex Differences in Performance and Rewards," *Academy of Management Journal* 58, no. 5 (2015): 1516–1545.

15. Richard F. Martell, David M. Lane, and Cynthia Emrich, "Male-Female Differences: A Computer Simulation," *American Psychologist* 51, no. 2 (1996): 157.

16. Monica Biernat, M. J. Tocci, and Joan C. Williams, "The Language of Performance Evaluations: Gender-Based Shifts in Content and Consistency of Judgment," *Social Psychological and Personality Science* 3, no. 2 (2012): 186–192.

17. Molly Carnes et al., "The Effect of an Intervention to Break the Gender Bias Habit for Faculty at One Institution: A Cluster Randomized, Controlled Trial," *Academic Medicine: Journal of the Association of American Medical Colleges* 90, no. 2 (2015): 221–230.

18. Taylor Campbell and Jamie Wescott, "Profile of Undergraduate Students: Attendance, Distance and Remedial Education, Degree Program and Field of Study, Demographics, Financial Aid, Financial Literacy, Employment, and Military Status: 2015–16," US Department of Education, 2019, https://nces.ed.gov/pubs2019/2019467.pdf.

Chapter 2

1. Alexandra Kalev, Frank Dobbin, and Erin Kelly, "Best Practices or Best Guesses? Assessing the Efficacy of Corporate Affirmative Action and Diversity Policies," *American Sociological Review* 71, no. 4 (2006): 589–617.

2. Frank Dobbin and Alexandra Kalev, "Why Doesn't Diversity Training Work? The Challenge for Industry and Academia," *Anthropology Now* 10, no. 2 (2018): 48–55.

3. Ibid.; Frank Dobbin and Alexandra Kalev, "Why Diversity Programs Fail," *Harvard Business Review*, July–August 2016, 52–60; Zachary T. Kalinoski et al., "A Meta-Analytic Evaluation of Diversity Training Outcomes," *Journal of Organizational Behavior* 34, no. 8 (2013): 1076–1104.

4. See also Evan P. Apfelbaum, Michael I. Norton, and Samuel R. Sommers, "Racial Colorblindness: Emergence, Practice, and Implications," *Psychological Science* 21 (2012): 205–209; Lisa Legault, Jennifer Gutsell, and Michael Inzlicht, "Ironic Effects of Antiprejudice Messages: How Motivational Interventions Can Reduce (but Also Increase) Prejudice," *Psychological Science* 22, no. 12 (2011): 1472–1477.

5. Jenny Roth, Roland Deutsch, and Jeffrey W. Sherman, "Automatic Antecedents of Discrimination," *European Psychologist* 24, no. 3 (2019).

6. Molly Carnes et al., "The Effect of an Intervention to Break the Gender Bias Habit for Faculty at One Institution: A Cluster Randomized, Controlled Trial," *Academic Medicine: Journal of the Association of American Medical Colleges* 90, no. 2 (2015): 221–230.

7. Patricia G. Devine et al., "A Gender Bias Habit-Breaking Intervention Led to Increased Hiring of Female Faculty in STEMM Departments," *Journal of Experimental Social Psychology* 73 (2017): 211–215.

8. Angela Lipsitz et al., "Counting on Blood Donors: Increasing the Impact of Reminder Calls," *Journal of Applied Social Psychology* 19, no. 13 (1989): 1057–1067; Githa Kanisin Overton and Ronald MacVicar, "Requesting a Commitment to Change: Conditions That Produce Behavioral or Attitudinal Commitment," *Journal of Continuing Education in the Health Professions* 28, no. 2 (2008): 60–66.

9. Zachary T. Kalinoski et al., "A Meta-Analytic Evaluation of Diversity Training Outcomes."

10. Carol T. Kulik and Loriann Roberson, "Diversity Initiative Effectiveness: What Organizations Can (and Cannot) Expect from Diversity Recruitment, Diversity Training, and Formal Mentoring Programs," in *Cambridge Companions to Management: Diversity at Work,*

ed. Arthur P. Brief (Cambridge: Cambridge University Press, 2008), 265–317.

11. Richard M. Ryan and Edward L. Deci, "Self-Determination Theory and the Facilitation of Intrinsic Motivation, Social Development, and Well-Being," *American Psychologist* 55, no. 1 (2000): 68–78.

12. Roy F. Baumeister, Laura Smart, and Joseph M. Boden, "Relation of Threatened Egotism to Violence and Aggression: The Dark Side of High Self-Esteem," *Psychological Review* 103, no. 1 (1996): 5–33.

13. Joan C. Williams et al., "Walking the Tightrope: An Examination of Bias in India's Engineering Workplace," Society of Women Engineers and the Center for WorkLife Law, 2018, https://worklifelaw.org/wp-content/uploads/2018/10/Walking-the-Tightrope-Bias-Indias-Engineering-Workplace.pdf; Joan C. Williams et al., "Climate Control: Gender and Racial Bias in Engineering?" Society of Women Engineers and the Center for WorkLife Law, 2016, https://worklifelaw.org/publications/Climate-Control-Gender-And-Racial-Bias-In-Engineering.pdf; Joan C. Williams, Katherine W. Phillips, and Erika V. Hall, "Double Jeopardy? Gender Bias Against Women of Color in Science," The Center for WorkLife Law, 2015, https://worklifelaw.org/publications/Double-Jeopardy-Report_v6_full_web-sm.pdf; Joan C. Williams et al., "You Can't Change What You Can't See: Interrupting Racial and Gender Bias in the Legal Profession," American Bar Association and Minority Corporate Counsel Association, 2018; Joan C. Williams, Rachel Korn, and Rachel Maas, "The Elephant in the (Well-Designed) Room: An Investigation into Bias in the Architecture Profession," The Center for WorkLife Law, forthcoming 2021.

14. Joan C. Williams, Rachel Korn, and Rachel Maas, "The Elephant in the (Well-Designed) Room."

15. Karissa Bell, "Google Chairman Gets Called Out for Cutting Off a Woman While Talking About Diversity," Mashable, March 16, 2015, https://mashable.com/2015/03/16/google-schmidt-unconscious-bias.

16. Jack Zenger and Joseph Folkman, "The Ideal Praise-to-Criticism Ratio," hbr.org, March 15, 2013, https://hbr.org/2013/03/the-ideal-praise-to-criticism.

17. Frank Dobbin and Alexandra Kalev, "Why Doesn't Diversity Training Work?"; Alexandra Kalev, Frank Dobbin, and Erin Kelly, "Best Practices or Best Guesses?"

18. Molly Carnes et al., "The Effect of an Intervention to Break the Gender Bias Habit for Faculty at One Institution: A Cluster Randomized, Controlled Trial."

19. Carol T. Kulik et al., "The Rich Get Richer: Predicting Participation in Voluntary Diversity Training," *Journal of Organizational*

Behavior: The International Journal of Industrial, Occupational and Organizational Psychology and Behavior 28, no. 6 (2007): 753–769.

20. Emilio J. Castilla, "Accounting for the Gap: A Firm Study Manipulating Organizational Accountability and Transparency in Pay Decisions," *Organization Science* 26, no. 2 (2015): 311–333.

Chapter 3

1. Gillian R. Brassil and Eleanor Lutz, "In 30 Years, Little Progress for U.S. Sports Leagues on Leadership Diversity," *The New York Times*, December 23, 2020, https://www.nytimes.com/interactive/2020/12/23/sports/diversity-coaches-sports.html?searchResultPosition=37.

2. Claudia Goldin and Cecilia Rouse, "Orchestrating Impartiality: The Impact of 'Blind' Auditions on Female Musicians," *American Economic Review* 90, no. 4 (2000): 715–741.

3. Katie R. Eyer, "That's Not Discrimination: American Beliefs and the Limits of Anti-Discrimination Law," *Minnesota Law Review* 96 (2011): 1275–1362.

4. Ibid.

5. Elizabeth L. Haines and John T. Jost, "Placating the Powerless: Effects of Legitimate and Illegitimate Explanation on Affect, Memory, and Stereotyping," *Social Justice Research* 13, no. 3 (2000): 219–236.

6. Katie R. Eyer, "That's Not Discrimination."

7. Gillian R. Brassil and Eleanor Lutz, "In 30 Years, Little Progress for U.S. Sports Leagues on Leadership Diversity."

8. Erin A. Cech, "The (Mis)Framing of Social Justice: Why Ideologies of Depoliticization and Meritocracy Hinder Engineers' Ability to Think about Social Injustices," in *Engineering Education for Social Justice: Philosophy of Engineering and Technology* vol. 10, edited by Juan Lucena (Dordrecht: Springer, 2013), 67–84.

9. Emilio J. Castilla and Stephen Benard, "The Paradox of Meritocracy in Organizations," *Administrative Science Quarterly* 55, no. 4 (2010): 543–576.

10. See, e.g., Andreas Leibbrandt and John A. List, "Do Women Avoid Salary Negotiations? Evidence from a Large Scale Natural Field Experiment," *Management Science* 61, no. 9 (2015): 2016–2024; for a good review of work on gender and behavioral economics, see: Iris Bohnet, "What Works: Gender Equality by Design," *Diplomatic Courier* 12, no. 2 (February 2018): 32–33, http://search.proquest.com/docview/2075501616.

11. Madeline E. Heilman, "Description and Prescription: How Gender Stereotypes Prevent Women's Ascent Up the Organizational

Ladder," *Journal of Social Issues* 57, no. 4 (2001): 657–674; Martha Foschi, "Double Standards in the Evaluation of Men and Women," *Social Psychology Quarterly* (1996): 237–254; Alice H. Eagly and Steven J. Karau, "Role Congruity Theory of Prejudice toward Female Leaders," *Psychological Review* 109, no. 3 (2002): 573–598; Cecilia L. Ridgeway, *Framed by Gender: How Gender Inequality Persists in the Modern World* (Oxford University Press, 2011); Victoria L. Brescoll, Erica Dawson, and Eric Luis Uhlmann, "Hard Won and Easily Lost: The Fragile Status of Leaders in Gender-Stereotype-Incongruent Occupations," *Psychological Science* 21, no. 11 (2010): 1640–1642.

12. Ed Yong, "The Transgender Scientist Who Changed Our Understanding of the Brain," *The Atlantic*, January 2, 2018, https://www.theatlantic.com/science/archive/2018/01/remembering-the-transgender-scientist-who-changed-our-understanding-of-the-brain/549458; Joan C. Williams and Rachel Dempsey, *What Works for Women at Work* (New York: New York University Press, 2014).

13. Linda L. Carli, "Interpersonal Relations and Group Processes," *Journal of Personality and Social Psychology* 59, no. 5 (1990): 941–951; Alice H. Eagly and Linda L. Carli, *Through the Labyrinth: The Truth About How Women Become Leaders* (Boston: Harvard Business Review Press, 2007); Cecilia L. Ridgeway, *Framed by Gender*; Victoria L. Brescoll, Erica Dawson, and Eric Luis Uhlmann, "Hard Won and Easily Lost."

14. Joan C. Williams, Katherine W. Phillips, and Erika V. Hall, "Double Jeopardy? Gender Bias Against Women of Color in Science," The Center for WorkLife Law, 2015, https://worklifelaw.org/publications/Double-Jeopardy-Report_v6_full_web-sm.pdf.

15. Joan C. Williams, Rachel Korn, and Rachel Maas, "The Elephant in the (Well-Designed) Room: An Investigation into Bias in the Architecture Profession," The Center for WorkLife Law, forthcoming 2021: 67, 70, 73.

16. Monica Biernat, M. J. Tocci, and Joan C. Williams, "The Language of Performance Evaluations: Gender-Based Shifts in Content and Consistency of Judgment," *Social Psychological and Personality Science* 3, no. 2 (2012): 186–192; Richard F. Martell, David M. Lane, and Cynthia Emrich, "Male-Female Differences: A Computer Simulation," *American Psychologist* 51, no. 2 (1996): 157.

17. For a good review, see: Robert W. Livingston, Ashleigh Shelby Rosette, and Ella F. Washington, "Can an Agentic Black Woman Get Ahead? The Impact of Race and Interpersonal Dominance on Perceptions of Female Leaders," *Psychological Science* 23, no. 4 (2012): 354–358; Shelley J. Correll, "Constraints into Preferences: Gender, Status, and Emerging Career Aspirations," *American Sociological Review*

69, no. 1 (2004): 93–113; Tristan L. Botelho and Mabel Abraham, "Pursuing Quality: How Search Costs and Uncertainty Magnify Gender-Based Double Standards in a Multistage Evaluation Process," *Administrative Science Quarterly* 62, no. 4 (2017): 698–730; Monica Biernat and Amanda K. Sesko, "Gender Stereotypes and Stereotyping," in *Gender, Sex, and Sexualities: Psychological Perspectives*, ed. Nancy K. Dess, Jeanne Marcek, and Leslie C. Bell (Oxford University Press, 2018): 171–194; Monica Biernat and Diane Kobrynowicz, "Gender- and Race-Based Standards of Competence: Lower Minimum Standards but Higher Ability Standards for Devalued Groups," *Journal of Personality and Social Psychology* 72, no. 3 (1997): 544–557.

18. Alice H. Eagly and Valerie J. Steffen, "Gender Stereotypes Stem from the Distribution of Women and Men into Social Roles," *Journal of Personality and Social Psychology* 46, no. 4 (1984): 735–754; Susan T. Fiske et al., "A Model of (Often Mixed) Stereotype Content: Competence and Warmth Respectively Follow from Perceived Status and Competition," *Journal of Personality and Social Psychology* 82, no. 6 (2002): 878–902; Madeline E. Heilman, Caryn J. Block, and Peter Stathatos, "The Affirmative Action Stigma of Incompetence: Effects of Performance Information Ambiguity," *Academy of Management Journal* 40, no. 3 (1997): 603–625.

19. Marilynn B. Brewer and Wendi Gardner, "Who Is This 'We'? Levels of Collective Identity and Self Representations," *Journal of Personality and Social Psychology* 71, no. 1 (1996): 83–93; Monica Biernat, Kathleen Fuegen, and Diane Kobrynowicz, "Shifting Standards and the Inference of Incompetence: Effects of Formal and Informal Evaluation Tools," *Personality and Social Psychology Bulletin* 36, no. 7 (2010): 855–868; Hannah Riley Bowles and Michele Gelfand, "Status and the Evaluation of Workplace Deviance," *Psychological Science* 21, no. 1 (2010): 49–54; Cara C. Bauer and Boris B. Baltes, "Reducing the Effects of Gender Stereotypes on Performance Evaluations," *Sex Roles* 47, no. 9 (2002): 465–476.

20. Arin N. Reeves, "Written in Black and White: Exploring Confirmation Bias in Racialized Perceptions of Writing Skills," Nextions, 2014, retrieved from http://nextions.com/wp-content/uploads/2017/05/written-in-black-and-white-yellow-paper-series.pdf.

21. Monica Biernat, Kathleen Fuegen, and Diane Kobrynowicz, "Shifting Standards and the Inference of Incompetence."

22. Joan C. Williams, Rachel Korn, and Rachel Maas, "The Elephant in the (Well-Designed) Room."

23. Kay Deaux and Tim Emswiller, "Explanations of Successful Performance on Sex-Linked Tasks: What Is Skill for the Male Is Luck for

the Female," *Journal of Personality and Social Psychology* 29, no. 1 (1974): 80–85; Marilynn B. Brewer, "In-Group Favoritism: The Subtle Side of Intergroup Discrimination," *Codes of Conduct: Behavioral Research and Business Ethics* (1996): 160–171.

24. Todd L. Pittinsky, Margaret Shih, and Nalini Ambady, "Will a Category Cue Affect You? Category Cues, Positive Reviewer Recall for Applicants," *Social Psychology of Education* 4, no. 1 (2000): 53–65.

25. Madeline E. Heilman and Michelle C. Haynes, "No Credit Where Credit Is Due: Attributional Rationalization of Women's Success in Male-Female Teams," *Journal of Applied Psychology* 90, no. 5 (2005): 905–916.

26. Joan C. Williams, Rachel Korn, and Rachel Maas, "The Elephant in the (Well-Designed) Room," 38.

27. Joseph G. Weber, "The Nature of Ethnocentric Bias: Ingroup Protection or Enhancement?" *Journal of Experimental Social Psychology* 30, no. 5 (1994): 482–504.

28. Marilynn B. Brewer, "In-Group Favoritism," 167.

29. Marilynn B. Brewer, "The Psychology of Prejudice: Ingroup Love and Outgroup Hate?" *Journal of Social Issues* 55, no. 3 (1999): 429–444.

30. Shelley J. Correll et al., "Inside the Black Gendered Performance Assessment," *American Sociological Review* 85, no. 6 (2020): 1022–1050.

31. Edward L. Thorndike, "A Constant Error in Psychological Ratings," *Journal of Applied Psychology* 4, no. 1 (1920): 25–29.

32. Heather Sarsons, "Rainfall and Conflict: A Cautionary Tale," *Journal of Development Economics* 115 (2015): 62–72; Michelle C. Haynes and Madeline E. Heilman, "It Had to Be You (Not Me)! Women's Attributional Rationalization of Their Contribution to Successful Joint Work Outcomes," *Personality and Social Psychology Bulletin* 39, no. 7 (2013): 956–969.

33. Michelle M. Duguid, Denise Lewin Loyd, and Pamela S. Tolbert, "The Impact of Categorical Status, Numeric Representation, and Work Group Prestige on Preference for Demographically Similar Others: A Value Threat Approach," *Organization Science* 23, no. 2 (2012): 386–401.

34. Christopher D. DeSante, "Working Twice as Hard to Get Half as Far: Race, Work Ethic, and America's Deserving Poor," *American Journal of Political Science* 57, no. 2 (2013): 342–356.

35. Cecilia L. Ridgeway, *Framed by Gender*; Monica Biernat and Diane Kobrynowicz, "Gender- and Race-Based Standards of Competence"; Corinne A. Moss-Racusin et al., "Science Faculty's Subtle Gender Biases Favor Male Students," *Proceedings of the National Academy of Sciences* 109, no. 41 (2012): 16474–16479; Mason Ameri et al.,

"The Disability Employment Puzzle: A Field Experiment on Employer Hiring Behavior," *ILR Review* 71, no. 2 (2018): 329–364; András Tilcsik, "Pride and Prejudice: Employment Discrimination Against Gay Men in the United States," *American Journal of Sociology* 117, no. 2 (2011): 586–626; Amy J. C. Cuddy, Michael I. Norton, and Susan T. Fiske, "This Old Stereotype: The Pervasiveness and Persistence of the Elderly Stereotype," *Journal of Social Issues* 61, no. 2 (2005): 267–285; Heather K. Davison and Michael J. Burke, "Sex Discrimination in Simulated Employment Contexts: A Meta-Analytic Investigation," *Journal of Vocational Behavior* 56, no. 2 (2000): 225–248; Alice H. Eagly and Linda L. Carli, *Through the Labyrinth*; Cecilia L. Ridgeway, "Gender, Status, and Leadership," *Journal of Social Issues* 57, no. 4 (2001): 637–655; Cecilia L. Ridgeway, "Status in Groups: The Importance of Motivation," *American Sociological Review* (1982): 76–88; Eva Derous and Jeroen Decoster, "Implicit Age Cues in Resumes: Subtle Effects on Hiring Discrimination," *Frontiers in Psychology* 8 (2017): 1321; Doris Weichselbaumer, "Discrimination Against Migrant Job Applicants in Austria: An Experimental Study," *German Economic Review* 18, no. 2 (2017): 237–265.

36. Joseph Berger, Bernard P. Cohen, and Morris Zelditch Jr., "Status Characteristics and Social Interaction," *American Sociological Review* (1972): 241–255.

37. Shelley J. Correll and Cecilia L. Ridgeway, "Expectation States Theory," in *Handbook of Social Psychology*, ed. John DeLamater (Boston: Springer, 2006): 29–51; Kimberle Crenshew, "Demarginalizing the Intersection of Race and Sex: A Black Feminist Critique of Antidiscrimination Doctrine, Feminist Theory and Antiracist Politics," in *University of Chicago Legal Forum* vol. 140, no. 1 (1989): 139–167; Patricia Hill Collins, *Black Feminist Thought: Knowledge, Consciousness, and the Politics of Empowerment,* 2nd ed. (Abingdon, UK: Routledge, 1999).

38. Ashleigh Shelby Rosette and Robert W. Livingston, "Failure Is Not an Option for Black Women: Effects of Organizational Performance on Leaders with Single versus Dual-Subordinate Identities," *Journal of Experimental Social Psychology* 48, no. 5 (September 2012): 1162–1167.

39. Robert W. Livingston, Ashleigh Shelby Rosette, and Ella F. Washington, "Can an Agentic Black Woman Get Ahead?"

40. Heather K. Davison and Michael J. Burke, "Sex Discrimination in Simulated Employment Contexts: A Meta-Analytic Investigation," *Journal of Vocational Behavior* 56, no. 2 (2000): 225–248; Alice H. Eagly and Linda L. Carli, *Through the Labyrinth*; Eva Derous and Jeroen Decoster, "Implicit Age Cues in Resumes: Subtle Effects on Hiring Discrimination"; Corinne A. Moss-Racusin et al., "Science Faculty's Subtle Gender Biases Favor Male Students."

41. Ibid.

42. Eric Luis Uhlmann and Geoffrey L. Cohen, "Constructed Criteria: Redefining Merit to Justify Discrimination," *Psychological Science* 16, no. 6 (2005): 474–480.

43. Marilynn B. Brewer, "In-group Favoritism."

44. Monica Biernat, M. J. Tocci, and Joan C. Williams, "The Language of Performance Evaluations."

45. Shelley J. Correll et al., "Inside the Black Box of Organizational Life," *American Sociological Review* 85, no. 6 (2020): 1022–1050.

46. Joan C. Williams, *Fair Measure: Toward Effective Attorney Evaluations,* 2nd ed. (Chicago: American Bar Association, 2008).

47. Shelley J. Correll, Katherine R. Weisshaar, Alison T. Wynn, and JoAnne Delfino Wehner, "Inside the Black Box of Organizational Life."

48. Marilynn B. Brewer and Wendi Gardner, "Who Is This 'We'?"; Monica Biernat, Kathleen Fuegen, and Diane Kobrynowicz, "Shifting Standards and the Inference of Incompetence"; Hannah Riley Bowles and Michele Gelfand, "Status and the Evaluation of Workplace Deviance"; Cara C. Bauer and Boris B. Baltes, "Reducing the Effects of Gender Stereotypes on Performance Evaluations."

49. Ben Schmidt, "Gendered Language in Teacher Reviews," 2015, https://benschmidt.org/profGender; Shelley J. Correll et al. "Inside the Black Box of Organizational Life"; Lauren A. Rivera and András Tilcsik, "Scaling Down Inequality: Rating Scales, Gender Bias, and the Architecture of Evaluation," *American Sociological Review* 84, no. 2 (2019): 248–274.

50. Bettina Casad, "Confirmation Bias," *Encyclopedia Britannica*, October 9, 2019, https://www.britannica.com/science/confirmation -bias.

51. Scott Simon, "Black Fraternity, Packed with Past Greats, Looks to Build Future Leaders," NPR, February 6, 2021, https://www.npr .org/2021/02/06/964764222/black-fraternity-packed-with-past-greats -looks-to-build-future-leaders.

52. Jennifer S. Lerner and Philip E. Tetlock, "Accounting for the Effects of Accountability," *Psychological Bulletin* 125, no. 2 (1999): 255–275.

Chapter 4

1. Erika V. Hall and Robert W. Livingston, "The Hubris Penalty: Biased Responses to 'Celebration' Displays of Black Players," *Journal of Experimental Social Psychology* 48, no. 4 (2012): 899–904.

2. Qian Julie Wang, "Anti-Asian Racism Isn't New." *New York Times*, February 18, 2021, https://www.nytimes.com/2021/02/18/opinion/asian-americans-racism.html.

3. Lincoln Quillian et al., "Meta-Analysis of Field Experiments Shows No Change in Discrimination in Hiring over Time," *Proceedings of the National Academy of Sciences* 114, no. 41 (2017): 10870–10875.

4. Suyeon Lee and Sara F. Waters, "Asians and Asian Americans' Experiences of Racial Discrimination During the COVID-19 Pandemic: Impacts on Health Outcomes and the Buffering Role of Social Support," *Stigma and Health* 6, no. 1 (2020): 70–78.

5. Laura Anthony, "Employee Suing United Airlines After Finding a Noose in His Work Area," ABC 7 News, September 11, 2014, https://abc7news.com/civil-rights-lawsuit-united-airlines-investigation/305135.

6. Joan C. Williams and Rachel Dempsey, *What Works for Women at Work* (New York: New York University Press, 2014).

7. Isabel Wilkerson, *Caste: The Origins of Our Discontents* (New York: Random House, 2020).

8. Amy J. C. Cuddy, Susan T. Fiske, and Peter Glick, "The BIAS Map: Behaviors from Intergroup Affect and Stereotypes," *Journal of Personality and Social Psychology* 92, no. 4 (2007): 631–648.; Susan T. Fiske et al., "A Model of (Often Mixed) Stereotype Content: Competence and Warmth Respectively Follow from Perceived Status and Competition," *Journal of Personality and Social Psychology* 82, no. 6 (2002): 878–902; Colin Ho and Jay W. Jackson, "Attitude Toward Asian Americans: Theory and Measurement," *Journal of Applied Social Psychology* 31, no. 8 (2001): 1553–1581; Jennifer L. Berdahl and Ji-A Min, "Prescriptive Stereotypes and Workplace Consequences for East Asians in North America," *Cultural Diversity and Ethnic Minority Psychology* 18, no. 2 (2012): 141–152.

9. Joan C. Williams, Katherine W. Phillips, and Erika V. Hall, "Double Jeopardy? Gender Bias Against Women of Color in Science," The Center for WorkLife Law, 2015, https://worklifelaw.org/publications/Double-Jeopardy-Report_v6_full_web-sm.pdf.

10. Janet E. Gans Epner, "Visible Invisibility: Women of Color in Law Firms," American Bar Assocation, 2006.

11. Aditi Vashist et al., "An Interdisciplinary Path for Intersectional Research," *Academy of Management Proceedings* (2019): 11342.

12. Joanna Almeida et al., "The Association Between Anti-immigrant Policies and Perceived Discrimination Among Latinos in the US: A Multilevel Analysis," *SSM Population Health* 2 (2016): 897–903.

13. Joan C. Williams, Katherine W. Phillips, and Erika V. Hall, "Double Jeopardy?"

14. Joan C. Williams and Rachel Dempsey, *What Works for Women at Work*.

15. Joan C. Williams, Rachel Korn, and Rachel Maas, "Pinning Down the Jellyfish: Women of Color in Tech," The Center for WorkLife Law, forthcoming 2021.

16. Cecilia L. Ridgeway and Sandra Nakagawa, "Is Deference the Price of Being Seen as Reasonable? How Status Hierarchies Incentivize Acceptance of Low Status," *Social Psychology Quarterly* 80, no. 2 (2017): 132–152; Cecilia Ridgeway, "A Painful Lesson in Why We Have to Take Status Seriously," Speak for Sociology, December 22, 2016, http://speak4sociology.org/author/cecilia-ridgeway.

17. Michelle C. Haynes and Madeline E. Heilman, "It Had to Be You (Not Me)! Women's Attributional Rationalization of Their Contribution to Successful Joint Work Outcomes," *Personality and Social Psychology Bulletin* 39, no. 7 (2013): 956–969.

18. See, e.g., Kathryn M. Bartol and D. Anthony Butterfield, "Sex Effects in Evaluating Leaders," *Journal of Applied Psychology* 61, no. 4 (1976): 446–454; Frances Cherry and Kay Deaux, "Fear of Success versus Fear of Gender-Inappropriate Behavior," *Sex Roles* 4, no. 1 (1978): 97–101; Laurie A. Rudman and Julie E. Phelan, "Backlash Effects for Disconfirming Gender Stereotypes in Organizations," *Research in Organizational Behavior* 28 (2008): 61–79; Laurie A. Rudman et al., "Status Incongruity and Backlash Effects: Defending the Gender Hierarchy Motivates Prejudice Against Female Leaders," *Journal of Experimental Social Psychology* 48, no. 1 (2012): 165–179; Victoria L. Brescoll and Eric Luis Uhlmann, "Can an Angry Woman Get Ahead? Status Conferral, Gender, and Expression of Emotion in the Workplace," *Psychological Science* 19, no. 3 (2008): 268–275; Alice H. Eagly and Steven J. Karau, "Role Congruity Theory of Prejudice Toward Female Leaders," *Psychological Review* 109, no. 3 (2002): 573–598; Tyler G. Okimoto and Victoria L. Brescoll, "The Price of Power: Power Seeking and Backlash Against Female Politicians," *Personality and Social Psychology Bulletin* 36, no. 7 (2010): 923–936; Laurie A. Rudman, "Self-Promotion as a Risk Factor for Women: The Costs and Benefits of Counterstereotypical Impression Management," *Journal of Personality and Social Psychology* 74, no. 3 (1998): 629–645; Laurie A. Rudman and Kimberly Fairchild, "Reactions to Counterstereotypic Behavior: The Role of Backlash in Cultural Stereotype Maintenance," *Journal of Personality and Social Psychology* 87, no. 2 (2004): 157–176; Laurie A. Rudman and Peter Glick, "Feminized Management and Backlash Toward Agentic Women: The Hidden Costs to Women of a Kinder, Gentler Image of

Middle Managers," *Journal of Personality and Social Psychology* 77, no. 5 (1999): 1,004–1,010; Laurie A. Rudman and Peter Glick, "Prescriptive Gender Stereotypes and Backlash Toward Agentic Women," *Journal of Social Issues* 57, no. 4 (2001): 743–762; Alice H. Eagly and Linda L. Carli, *Through the Labyrinth: The Truth About How Women Become Leaders* (Boston: Harvard Business Review Press, 2007); Madeline E. Heilman et al., "Penalties for Success: Reactions to Women Who Succeed at Male Gender-Typed Tasks," *Journal of Applied Psychology* 89, no. 3 (2004): 416.

19. Cecilia L. Ridgeway, "Gender, Status, and Leadership," *Journal of Social Issues* 57, no. 4 (2001): 637–655.

20. Alice H. Eagly and Steven J. Karau, "Role Congruity Theory of Prejudice Toward Female Leaders"; Susan T. Fiske et al., "A Model of (Often Mixed) Stereotype Content."

21. Joan C. Williams, Katherine W. Phillips, and Erika V. Hall, "Double Jeopardy?"

22. Ibid.

23. Joan C. Williams, Rachel Korn, and Rachel Maas, "The Elephant in the (Well-Designed) Room: An Investigation into Bias in the Architecture Profession," The Center for WorkLife Law, forthcoming 2021.

24. Joan C. Williams and Rachel Dempsey, *What Works for Women at Work*; Deborah Gruenfeld, "Power & Influence," Stanford Graduate School of Business, YouTube video, http://youtu.be/KdQHAeAnHmw; see also: Laurie A. Rudman and Julie E. Phelan, "Backlash Effects for Disconfirming Gender Stereotypes in Organizations," *Research in Organizational Behavior* 28 (2008): 61–79.

25. Olivia A. O'Neill and Charles A. O'Reilly III, "Reducing the Backlash Effect: Self-Monitoring and Women's Promotions," *Journal of Occupational and Organizational Psychology* 84, no. 4 (2011): 825–832.

26. Christopher F. Karpowitz, Tali Mendelberg, and Lee Shaker, "Gender Inequality in Deliberative Participation," *American Political Science Review* 106, no. 3 (2012): 533–547.

27. Justin McCurry, "Tokyo 2020 Chief Pressed to Resign After Saying Women Talked Too Much at Meetings," *The Guardian*, February 3, 2021, https://www.theguardian.com/sport/2021/feb/04/tokyo-2020-chief-pressed-to-resign-after-saying-women-talked-too-much-at-meetings.

28. Motoko Rich, "After Leader's Sexist Remark, Tokyo Olympics Makes Symbolic Shift," *New York Times*, February 18, 2021, https://www.nytimes.com/2021/02/18/world/asia/yoshiro-mori-tokyo-olympics-seiko-hashimoto.html.

29. Michael Argyle, Mansur Lalljee, and Mark Cook, "The Effects of Visibility on Interaction in a Dyad," *Human Relations* 21, no. 1 (1968): 3–17; Anthony Mulac et al., "Male/Female Language Differences and Effects in Same-Sex and Mixed-Sex Dyads: The Gender-Linked Language Effect," *Communications Monographs* 55, no. 4 (1988): 315–335; Don Zimmerman and Candace West, "Sex Roles, Interruptions, and Silences in Conversations," in *Language and Sex: Difference and Dominance*, eds. Barrie Thorne and Nancy Henley (Rowley, MA: Newbury House, 1975); Cecilia L. Ridgeway and Joseph Berger, "Expectations, Legitimation, and Dominance Behavior in Task Groups," *American Sociological Review* (1986): 603–617; Faye Crosby and Linda Nyquist, "The Female Register: An Empirical Study of Lakoff's Hypotheses," *Language in Society* 6, no. 3 (1977): 313–322; Albert O. Hirschman and Michael Rothschild, "The Changing Tolerance for Income Inequality in the Course of Economic Development," *Quarterly Journal of Economics* 87, no. 4 (1973): 544–566.

30. Pascaline Dupas et al., "Gender and the Dynamics of Economics Seminars," working paper 28494, National Bureau of Economic Research, 2021.

31. Robert W. Livingston, Ashleigh Shelby Rosette, and Ella F. Washington, "Can an Agentic Black Woman Get Ahead? The Impact of Race and Interpersonal Dominance on Perceptions of Female Leaders," *Psychological Science* 23, no. 4 (2012): 354–358; Erika V. Hall and Robert W. Livingston, "The Hubris Penalty."

32. Jennifer L. Berdahl and Ji-A Min, "Prescriptive Stereotypes and Workplace Consequences for East Asians in North America."

33. Victoria L. Brescoll and Eric Luis Uhlmann, "Can an Angry Woman Get Ahead?"

34. Monica Biernat and Amanda K. Sesko, "Gender Stereotypes and Stereotyping," in *Gender, Sex, and Sexualities: Psychological Perspectives*, eds. Nancy Dess, Jeanne Marecek, and Leslie Bell (Oxford University Press, 2018): 171–194; Victoria L. Brescoll, "Leading with Their Hearts? How Gender Stereotypes of Emotion Lead to Biased Evaluations of Female Leaders," *Leadership Quarterly* 27, no. 3 (2016): 415–428; Stephanie A. Shields, "Gender and Emotion: What We Think We Know, What We Need to Know, and Why It Matters," *Psychology of Women Quarterly* 37, no. 4 (2013): 423–435.

35. Jessica M. Salerno and Liana C. Peter-Hagene, "One Angry Woman: Anger Expression Increases Influence for Men, but Decreases Influence for Women, During Group Deliberation," *Law and Human Behavior* 39, no. 6 (2015): 581–592.

36. Leah D. Sheppard and Karl Aquino, "Much Ado About Nothing? Observers' Problematization of Women's Same-Sex Conflict at Work," *Academy of Management Perspectives* 27, no. 1 (2013): 52–62.

37. Madeline E. Heilman and Julie J. Chen, "Same Behavior, Different Consequences: Reactions to Men's and Women's Altruistic Citizenship Behavior," *Journal of Applied Psychology* 90, no. 3 (2005): 431–441; Tammy D. Allen, "Rewarding Good Citizens: The Relationship Between Citizenship Behavior, Gender, and Organizational Rewards," *Journal of Applied Social Psychology* 36, no. 1 (2006): 120–143.

38. Holly English, *Gender on Trial: Sexual Stereotypes and Work/Life Balance in the Legal Workplace* (New York: ALM Publishing, 2003).

39. Shelley J. Correll et al., "Inside the Black Box of Organizational Life: The Gendered Language of Performance Assessment," *American Sociological Review* 85, no. 6 (2020): 1022–1050.

40. Monica Biernat, M. J. Tocci, and Joan C. Williams, "The Language of Performance Evaluations: Gender-Based Shifts in Content and Consistency of Judgment," *Social Psychological and Personality Science* 3, no. 2 (2012): 186–192.

41. Ibid.

42. Lisa Sinclair and Ziva Kunda, "Motivated Stereotyping of Women: She's Fine If She Praised Me but Incompetent If She Criticized Me," *Personality and Social Psychology Bulletin* 26, no. 11 (2000): 1329–1342.

43. Melissa C. Thomas-Hunt and Katherine W. Phillips, "When What You Know Is Not Enough: Expertise and Gender Dynamics in Task Groups," *Personality and Social Psychology Bulletin* 30, no. 12 (2004): 1585–1598.

44. Susan Shackelford, Wendy Wood, and Stephen Worchel, "Behavioral Styles and the Influence of Women in Mixed-Sex Groups," *Social Psychology Quarterly* (1996): 284–293; Cecilia L. Ridgeway, "Status in Groups: The Importance of Motivation," *American Sociological Review* (1982): 76–88; Barbara Westbrook Eakins and Rollin Gene Eakins, *Sex Differences in Human Communication* (Boston: Houghton Mifflin School, 1978); Bennett J. Tepper, Sheryl J. Brown, and Marilyn D. Hunt, "Strength of Subordinates' Upward Influence Tactics and Gender Congruency Effects," *Journal of Applied Social Psychology* 23, no. 22 (1993): 1903–1919; Cecilia L. Ridgeway and Joseph Berger, "Expectations, Legitimation, and Dominance Behavior in Task Groups," *American Sociological Review* (1986): 603–617; Faye Crosby and Linda Nyquist, "The Female Register: An Empirical Study of Lakoff's Hypotheses"; Albert O. Hirschman and Michael Rothschild, "The

Changing Tolerance for Income Inequality in the Course of Economic Development"; E. Holly Buttner and Martha McEnally, "The Interactive Effect of Influence Tactic, Applicant Gender, and Type of Job on Hiring Recommendations," *Sex Roles* 34, no. 7–8 (1996): 581–591.

45. Melissa C. Thomas-Hunt and Katherine W. Phillips, "When What You Know Is Not Enough: Expertise and Gender Dynamics in Task Groups."

46. Pascaline Dupas et al., "Gender and the Dynamics of Economics Seminars," working paper 28494, National Bureau of Economic Research, 2021.

Chapter 5

1. Joan C. Williams et al., "Climate Control: Gender and Racial Bias in Engineering?" Society of Women Engineers and the Center for WorkLife Law, 2016, https://worklifelaw.org/publications/Climate -Control-Gender-And-Racial-Bias-In-Engineering.pdf; Joan C. Williams et al., "You Can't Change What You Can't See: Interrupting Racial and Gender Bias in the Legal Profession," American Bar Association and Minority Corporate Counsel Association, 2018.

2. Ian M. Handley et al., "Quality of Evidence Revealing Subtle Gender Biases in Science Is in the Eye of the Beholder," *Proceedings of the National Academy of Sciences* 112, no. 43 (2015): 13201–13206.

3. Erin A. Cech, "The (Mis)Framing of Social Justice: Why Ideologies of Depoliticization and Meritocracy Hinder Engineers' Ability to Think About Social Injustices," in *Engineering Education for Social Justice: Philosophy of Engineering and Technology*, vol. 10., ed. Juan Lucena (Dordrecht: Springer, 2013), 67–84.

4. Joan C. Williams,*White Working Class: Overcoming Class Cluelessness in America* (Boston: Harvard Business Review Press, 2017); Joan C. Williams, "What So Many People Don't Get About the U.S. Working Class," hbr.org, November 10, 2016, https://hbr.org /2016/11/what-so-many-people-dont-get-about-the-u-s-working-class.

5. Tamara Draut, "Understanding the Working Class," Demos, April 16, 2018, https://www.demos.org/research/understanding -working-class.

6. Joan C. Williams, *Reshaping the Work-Family Debate: Why Men and Class Matter* (Boston: Harvard University Press, 2010).

7. Ronald S. Burt,*Structural Holes* (Boston: Harvard University Press, 1992).

8. Joan C. Williams, *White Working Class*; Peter Belmi and Kristin Laurin, "Who Wants to Get to the Top? Class and Lay Theories About

Power," *Journal of Personality and Social Psychology* 111, no. 4 (2016): 505–529.

9. For a good review of the literature, see Peter Belmi et al., "The Social Advantage of Miscalibrated Individuals: The Relationship Between Social Class and Overconfidence and Its Implications for Class-Based Inequality," *Journal of Personality and Social Psychology* 118, no. 2 (2020): 254–282.

10. Peter Belmi and Kristin Laurin, "Who Wants to Get to the Top?"; Nicole M. Stephens et al., "A Cultural Mismatch: Independent Cultural Norms Produce Greater Increases in Cortisol and More Negative Emotions Among First-Generation College Students," *Journal of Experimental Social Psychology* 48, no. 6 (2012): 1389–1393.

11. Joan C. Williams, *White Working Class.*

12. Daniel Laurison and Sam Friedman, "The Class Pay Gap in Higher Professional and Managerial Occupations," *American Sociological Review* 81, no. 4 (2016): 668–695.

13. Nicole M. Stephens et al., "Social-Class Disparities in Higher Education and Professional Workplaces: The Role of Cultural Mismatch," *Current Directions in Psychological Science* 28, no. 1 (2019): 67–73.

14. Paul Ingram and Jean Joohyun Oh, "Mapping the Class Ceiling: The Social Class Disadvantage for Attaining Management Positions," *Academy of Management Discoveries* (2020).

15. Ibid.

16. RTI International, "First Generation College Students: Demographic Characteristics and Post-Secondary Enrollment," Washington, DC: NASPA, 2019, https://firstgen.naspa.org/research-and -policy/national-data-fact-sheets-on-first-generation-college-students /national-data-fact-sheets.

17. Paul Ingram and Jean Joohyun Oh, "Mapping the Class Ceiling."

18. Ibid.

19. Richard A. Posthuma, Maria Fernanda Wagstaff, and Michael A. Campion, "Age Stereotypes and Workplace Age Discrimination: A Framework for Future Research," in *Oxford Library of Psychology. The Oxford Handbook of Work and Aging*, eds. J. W. Hedge amd W. C. Borman (Oxford University Press, 2012), 298–312, https://doi.org/10.1093/ oxfordhb/9780195385052.013.0104.

20. Laurie A. Rudman, "Self-Promotion as a Risk Factor for Women: The Costs and Benefits of Counterstereotypical Impression Management," *Journal of Personality and Social Psychology* 74, no. 3 (1998): 629–654; Laurie A. Rudman and Peter Glick, "Feminized Management and Backlash Toward Agentic Women: The Hidden Costs to Women of a Kinder, Gentler Image of Middle Managers," *Journal of Personality*

and Social Psychology 77, no. 5 (1999): 1004–1010; Laurie A. Rudman and Peter Glick, "Prescriptive Gender Stereotypes and Backlash Toward Agentic Women," *Journal of Social Issues* 57, no. 4 (2001): 743–762.

21. Kenneth Matos, Olivia O'Neill, and Xue Lei, "Toxic Leadership and the Masculinity Contest Culture: How 'Win or Die' Cultures Breed Abusive Leadership," *Journal of Social Issues* 74, no. 3 (2018): 500–528.

22. Joan C. Williams, *White Working Class*; Michael H. Bond, Kwok Leung, and Kwok Choi Wan, "How Does Cultural Collectivism Operate? The Impact of Task and Maintenance Contributions on Reward Distribution," *Journal of Cross-Cultural Psychology* 13, no. 2 (1982): 186–200; Huajian Cai et al., "Tactical Self-Enhancement in China: Is Modesty at the Service of Self-Enhancement in East Asian Culture?" *Social Psychological and Personality Science* 2, no. 1 (2011): 59–64.

23. Lauren Rivera and András Tilcsik, "Research: How Subtle Class Cues Can Backfire on Your Resume," hbr.org, December 21, 2016, https://hbr.org/2016/12/research-how-subtle-class-cues-can-backfire-on-your-resume.

24. Joan C. Williams, Marina Multhaup, and Sky Mihaylo, "Why Companies Should Add Class to Their Diversity Discussions," hbr.org, September 5, 2018, https://hbr.org/2018/09/why-companies-should-add-class-to-their-diversity-discussions.

25. Raj Chetty et al., "Mobility Report Cards: The Role of Colleges in Intergenerational Mobility," working paper 23618, National Bureau of Economic Research, 2017.

26. Joan C. Williams, *White Working Class*.

27. Joan C. Williams, Marina Multhaup, and Sky Mihaylo, "Why Companies Should Add Class to Their Diversity Discussions."

28. Laszlo Bock, *Work Rules!* (New York: Twelve, 2015), 12.

29. Peter Belmi et al., "The Social Advantage of Miscalibrated Individuals," *Journal of Personality and Social Psychology* 118, no. 2 (February 2020): 254–282.

30. Atul Gawande, *Complications: A Surgeon's Notes on an Imperfect Science* (New York: Metropolitan Books, 2003).

31. Stephanie K. Johnson and David R. Hekman, "Women and Minorities Are Penalized for Promoting Diversity," hbr.org, March 23, 2016, https://hbr.org/2016/03/women-and-minorities-are-penalized-for-promoting-diversity.

32. EY, "Women on US Boards: What Are We Seeing?" 2015, https://www.diversityincbestpractices.com/medialib/uploads/2015/02/EY-women-on-us-boards-what-are-we-seeing.pdf.

33. David Gelles, "'There Is a Bigger Role': A C.E.O. Pushes Diversity," *New York Times*, March 5, 2021, https://www.nytimes.com/2021/03/05/business/tim-ryan-pwc-corner-office.html.

Chapter 6

1. Lauren A. Rivera, "Hiring as Cultural Matching: The Case of Elite Professional Service Firms," *American Sociological Review* 77, no. 6 (2012): 999–1022.

2. Rick Torben, "How and Why Organizational Culture Eats Strategy for Breakfast, Lunch and Dinner," SupplyChair247, February 27, 2020, https://www.supplychain247.com/article/organizational_culture_eats_strategy_for_breakfast_lunch_and_dinner.

3. Lauren A. Rivera, "Hiring as Cultural Matching."

4. Ibid.

5. David Rock, Heidi Grant, and Jacqui Grey, "Diverse Teams Feel Less Comfortable—and That's Why They Perform Better," hbr.org, September 22, 2016, https://hbr.org/2016/09/diverse-teams-feel-less-comfortable-and-thats-why-they-perform-better.

6. Laszlo Bock, *Work Rules!* (New York: Twelve, 2015), 12.

7. Mary Meisenzahl, "Google Made a Small but Important Change in 2017 to How It Thinks About 'Googleyness,' A Key Value It Looks for In New Hires," Business Insider, October 31, 2019, https://www.businessinsider.com/google-googleyness-hiring-training-guide-change-2019-10.

8. Devon W. Carbado and Mitu Gulati, *Acting White? Rethinking Race in Post-Racial America* (Oxford University Press, 2013).

9. Robert W. Livingston and Nicholas A. Pearce, "The Teddy-Bear Effect: Does Having a Baby Face Benefit Black Chief Executive Officers?" *Psychological Science* 20, no. 10 (2009): 1229–1236.

10. Jennifer L. Berdahl, Peter Glick, and Marianne Cooper, "How Masculinity Contests Undermine Organizations, and What to Do About It," hbr.org, November 2, 2018, https://hbr.org/2018/11/how-masculinity-contests-undermine-organizations-and-what-to-do-about-it.

11. Joan C. Williams, Rachel Korn, and Rachel Maas, "Pinning Down the Jellyfish: Women of Color in Tech," The Center for WorkLife Law, forthcoming 2021.

12. Peter Glick, Jennifer L. Berdahl, and Natalya M. Alonso, "Development and Validation of the Masculinity Contest Culture Scale," *Journal of Social Issues* 74, no. 3 (2018): 449–476.

13. Ibid.

14. Amy C. Edmondson and Zhike Lei, "Psychological Safety: The History, Renaissance, and Future of an Interpersonal Construct," *Annual Review of Organizational Psychology and Organizational Behavior* 1, no. 1 (2014): 23–43.

15. Christin L. Munsch et al., "Everybody Me: Pluralistic Ignorance and the Contest," *Journal of Social Issues* 74, no. 3 (2018): 551–578.

16. Erin Meyer, "Why Getting Drunk Is So Important in Japanese Business Relations," Business Insider, February 25, 2015, https://www.businessinsider.com/getting-drunk-in-japan-business-deals-2015-2.

17. Samuel B. Bacharach, Peter A. Bamberger, and Valerie M. McKinney, "Harassing Under the Influence: The Prevalence of Male Heavy Drinking, the Embeddedness of Permissive Workplace Drinking Norms, and the Gender Harassment of Female Coworkers," *Journal of Occupational Health Psychology* 12, no. 3 (2007): 232.

18. Jennifer L. Berdahl and Jana L. Raver, "Sexual Harassment," in *APA Handbook of Industrial and Organizational Psychology*, vol. 3, ed. Sheldon Zedeck (APA Books, 2011), 641–669.

19. Victoria L. Brescoll and Eric Luis Uhlmann, "Can an Angry Woman Get Ahead? Status Conferral, Gender, and Expression of Emotion in the Workplace," *Psychological Science* 19, no. 3 (2008): 268–275.

20. Lilia M. Cortina et al., "Selective Incivility as Modern Discrimination in Organizations: Evidence and Impact," *Journal of Management* 39, no. 6 (2013): 1579–1605.

21. "Golf Industry Facts," National Golf Foundation, 2019, https://www.ngf.org/golf-industry-research.

22. Pierre Bourdieu, *Distinction: A Social Critique of the Judgement of Taste* (Boston: Harvard University Press, 1984).

23. Kenji Yoshino, *Covering: The Hidden Assault on Our Civil Rights* (New York: Random House, 2011).

Chapter 7

1. Stephanie K. Johnson and David R. Hekman, "Women and Minorities Are Penalized for Promoting Diversity," hbr.org, March 23, 2016, https://hbr.org/2016/03/women-and-minorities-are-penalized-for-promoting-diversity.

2. Ronald S. Burt, *Structural Holes* (Boston: Harvard University Press, 1992).

3. Lisa E. Cohen, Joseph P. Broschak, and Heather A. Haveman, "And Then There Were More? The Effect of Organizational Sex Composition on the Hiring and Promotion of Managers," *American Sociological Review* (1998): 711–727.

4. Emilio J. Castilla and Stephen Benard, "The Paradox of Meritocracy in Organizations," *Administrative Science Quarterly* 55, no. 4 (2010): 543–576.

5. Lauren A. Rivera and András Tilcsik, "Class Advantage, Commitment Penalty: The Gendered Effect of Social Class Signals in an Elite Labor Market," *American Sociological Review* 81, no. 6 (2016): 1097–1131.

6. Joan C. Williams and Veta Richardson, "New Millennium, Same Glass Ceiling: The Impact of Law Firm Compensation Systems on Women," *Hastings Law Journal* 62 (2010): 597.

7. Joan C. Williams et al., "You Can't Change What You Can't See: Interrupting Racial and Gender Bias in the Legal Profession," American Bar Association and Minority Corporate Counsel Association, 2018, 101–104.

8. Meghan Rose Dickey, "Salesforce Has Spent About $6 Million to Fix Its Gender and Racial Pay Gap," TechCrunch, April 4, 2017, https://social.techcrunch.com/2017/04/04/salesforce-has-spent-about-6-million-to-fix-its-gender-and-racial-pay-gap-since-2015.

Chapter 8

1. Corinne A. Moss-Racusin, Aneta K. Molenda, and Charlotte R. Cramer, "Can Evidence Impact Attitudes? Public Reactions to Evidence of Gender Bias in STEM Fields," *Psychology of Women Quarterly* 39, no. 2 (2015): 194–209.

2. Shelley J. Correll, Stephen Benard, and In Paik, "Getting a Job: Is There a Motherhood Penalty?" *American Journal of Sociology* 112, no. 5 (2007): 1297–1338.

3. Faye J. Crosby, Joan C. Williams, and Monica Biernat, "The Maternal Wall," *Journal of Social Issues* 60, no. 4 (2004): 675–682.

4. Shelley J. Correll, Stephen Benard, and In Paik, "Getting a Job: Is There a Motherhood Penalty?"

5. Rebecca Glauber, "Trends in the Motherhood Wage Penalty and Fatherhood Wage Premium for Low, Middle, and High Earners," *Demography* 55, no. 5 (2018): 1663–1680.

6. Joan C. Williams, Rachel Korn, and Rachel Maas, "The Elephant in the (Well-Designed) Room: An Investigation into Bias in the Architecture Profession," The Center for WorkLife Law, forthcoming 2021, 47.

7. Janet E. Gans Epner, "Visible Invisibility: Women of Color in Law Firms," American Bar Assocation, 2006.

8. Stephen Benard and Shelley J. Correll, "Normative Discrimination and the Motherhood Penalty," *Gender and Society* 24, no. 5 (2010): 616–646.

9. Bostock v. Clayton County, 139 S. Ct. 2049 (2020); Back v. Hastings on Hudson Union Free School Dist., 365 F. 3d 107 (Court of Appeals, 2nd Circuit 2004).

10. Calvert T. Calvert, "Caregivers in the Workplace: Family Responsibilities Discrimination Litigation Update 2016," The Center for Worklife Law, 2016, 1–48.

11. Joan Williams et al., eds., *The Flexibility Stigma* (Hoboken, NJ: Wiley-Blackwell, 2013).

12. Laurie A. Rudman and Kris Mescher, "Penalizing Men Who Request a Family Leave: Is Flexibility Stigma a Femininity Stigma?" *Journal of Social Issues* 69, no. 2 (2013): 322–340.

13. Joseph A. Vandello et al., "When Equal Isn't Really Equal: The Masculine Dilemma of Seeking Work Flexibility," *Journal of Social Issues* 69, no. 2 (2013): 303–321.

14. Ibid.

15. The Family and Medical Leave Act, 29 CFR §825 (2013), https://www.govinfo.gov/content/pkg/FR-2013-02-06/pdf/2013-02383.pdf.

16. The United States Census Bureau, "Fertility of Women in the United States: 2018," https://www.census.gov/data/tables/2018/demo/fertility/women-fertility.html.

17. Marian Berelowitz and Nick Ayala, "The State of Men," JWT Intelligence, June 5, 2013, https://intelligence.wundermanthompson.com/2013/06/the-state-of-men.

18. Amy J. C. Cuddy, Susan T. Fiske, and Peter Glick, "When Professionals Become Mothers, Warmth Doesn't Cut the Ice," *Journal of Social Issues* 60, no. 4 (2004): 701–718; Jennifer L. Berdahl and Sue H. Moon, "Workplace Mistreatment of Middle Class Workers Based on Sex, Parenthood, and Caregiving," *Journal of Social Issues* 69, no. 2 (2013): 341–366.

19. Joni Hersch, "Opting Out Among Women with Elite Education," *Review of Economics of the Household* 11, no. 4 (2013): 469–506; Claudia Goldin and Joshua Mitchell, "The New Life Cycle of Women's Employment: Disappearing Humps, Sagging Middles, Expanding Tops," *Journal of Economic Perspectives* 31, no. 1 (2017): 161–182; Mary Blair-Loy, *Competing Devotions: Career and Family Among Women Executives* (Boston: Harvard University Press, 2009).

20. Joni Hersch and Jennifer Bennett Shinall, "Something to Talk About: Information Exchange Under Employment Law," *University of Pennsylvania Law Review* 165 (2016).

21. The American Institute of Architects, "Diversity in the Profession of Architecture," 2018, http://content.aia.org/sites/default/files/2016-05/Diversity-DiversityinArchitecture.pdf.

22. Joan C. Williams and Heather Boushey, "The Three Faces of Work-Family Conflict," Center for American Progress, 2010, https://www.americanprogress.org/issues/economy/reports/2010/01/25/7194/the-three-faces-of-work-family-conflict.

Chapter 9

1. Erin L. Kelly and Phyllis Moen, *Overload: How Good Jobs Went Bad and What We Can Do About It* (Princeton University Press, 2020).

2. G&A Partners, "Calculating the Cost of Employee Turnover," 2016, https://www.gnapartners.com/resources/articles/how-much-does-employee-turnover-really-cost-your-business.

3. Ellen Galinsky, "The New Male Mystique—It's No Joke!" *Huffington Post*, September 4, 2011, https://www.huffpost.com/entry/the-new-male-mystiqueits-_b_888900.

4. Irene Padavic, Robin J. Ely, and Erin M. Reid, "Explaining the Persistence of Gender Inequality: The Work–Family Narrative as a Social Defense Against the 24/7 Work Culture," *Administrative Science Quarterly* 65, no. 1 (2020): 61–111.

5. Leslie Perlow, *Finding Time: How Corporations, Individuals, and Families Can Benefit from New Work Practices* (Cornell University Press, 1997); Rhona Rapoport et al., *Beyond Work-Family Balance: Advancing Gender Equity and Workplace Performance* (San Francisco: Jossey-Bass, 2001).

6. Michèle Lamont, *Money, Morals, and Manners: The Culture of the French and the American Upper-Middle Class* (University of Chicago Press, 1992).

7. Mary Blair-Loy, *Competing Devotions: Career and Family Among Women Executives* (Harvard University Press, 2009); Mary Blair-Loy and Amy S. Wharton, "Mothers in Finance: Surviving and Thriving," *Annals of the American Academy of Political and Social Science* 596, no. 1 (2004): 151–171.

8. Ibid.

9. Joan C. Williams, *Reshaping the Work-Family Debate: Why Men and Class Matter* (Boston: Harvard University Press, 2010).

10. Cynthia Fuchs Epstein et al., *The Part-Time Paradox: Time Norms, Professional Life, Family, and Gender* (Routledge, 2014).

11. Marianne Cooper, "Being the 'Go-To Guy': Fatherhood, Masculinity, and the Organization of Work in Silicon Valley," *Qualitative Sociology* 23, no. 4 (2000): 37–405.

12. Erin Reid, "Embracing, Passing, Revealing, and the Ideal Worker Image: How People Navigate Expected and Experienced

Professional Identities," *Organization Science* 26, no. 4 (2015): 997–1017; Katherine C. Kellogg, *Challenging Operations: Medical Reform and Resistance in Surgery* (University of Chicago Press, 2011); Joan C. Williams, *Unbending Gender: Why Family and Work Conflict and What to Do About It* (Oxford University Press, 1999).

13. Cooper, "Being the 'Go-To Guy.'"

14. Irene Padavic, Robin J. Ely, and Erin M. Reid, "Explaining the Persistence of Gender Inequality."

15. Ibid.

16. Lotte Bailyn, *Breaking the Mold: Redesigning Work for Productive and Satisfying Lives*, 2nd ed. (Ithaca, NY: ILR Press, 2006); Erin L. Kelly and Phyllis Moen, *Overload*.

17. Youngjoo Cha, "Overwork and the Persistence of Gender Segregation in Occupations," *Gender and Society* 27, no. 2 (2013): 158–184.

18. Youngjoo Cha, "The Wage Premium for Working Long Hours Has Helped Lead to the Stagnation of the Gender Wage Gap," USAPP, https://blogs.lse.ac.uk/usappblog/2014/05/28/the-wage-premium-for -working-long-hours-has-helped-lead-to-the-stagnation-of-the-gender -wage-gap; Youngjoo Cha and Kim A. Weeden, "Overwork and the Slow Convergence in the Gender Gap in Wages," *American Sociological Review* 79, no. 3 (2014): 457–484.

19. Youngjoo Cha and Kim A. Weeden, "Overwork and the Slow Convergence in the Gender Gap in Wages."

20. Ibid.

21. Data generated by Rachel Korn, Director of Research on Organization Bias at WorkLife Law, based on the US Census Bureau's American Community Survey, 2021, retrieved from https://data.census .gov/cedsci.

22. Kids Count Data Center, "Children in Single-Parent Families by Race in the United States," 2020, https://datacenter.kidscount.org/data /tables/107-children-in-single-parent-families-by-race.

23. Julie Sullivan, "Comparing Characteristics and Selected Expenditures of Dual- and Single-Income Households with Children: Monthly Labor Review: U.S. Bureau of Labor Statistics," September 2020, https://www.bls.gov/opub/mlr/2020/article/comparing-characteristics -and-selected-expenditures-of-dual-and-single-income-households-with -children.htm; Youngjoo Cha, "Overwork and the Persistence of Gender Segregation in Occupations"; Samuel Stebbins and Evan Comen, "How Much Do You Need to Make to Be in the Top 1% in Every State? Here's the List," *USA Today*, July 1, 2020, https://www.usatoday.com/story

/money/2020/07/01/how-much-you-need-to-make-to-be-in-the-1-in
-every-state/112002276.

24. Jill E. Yavorsky, Lisa A. Keister, Yue Qian, "Gender in the One
Percent," *Contexts* 19, no. 1 (February 2020): 12–17.

25. PwC, "Business Needs a Tighter Strategy for Remote Work,"
January 12, 2021, https://www.pwc.com/us/en/library/covid-19
/us-remote-work-survey.html.

26. Nicholas Bloom et al., "Does Working from Home Work?
Evidence from a Chinese Experiment," *Quarterly Journal of Economics* 130,
no. 1 (2015): 165–218.

27. Olivier N. Godart, Holger Görg, and Aoife Hanley, "Trust-
Based Work Time and Innovation: Evidence from Firm-Level Data,"
ILR Review 70, no. 4 (October 2017): 894–918.

Chapter 10

1. August Wilson, *Ma Rainey's Black Bottom,* 1982.

2. Kemp Powers, *One Night in Miami . . .* , 2013.

3. Stephanie K. Johnson and David R. Hekman, "Women and
Minorities Are Penalized for Promoting Diversity," hbr.org, March 23,
2016, https://hbr.org/2016/03/women-and-minorities-are-penalized
-for-promoting-diversity; David R. Hekman et al., "Does Diversity-
Valuing Behavior Result in Diminished Performance Ratings for Non-
White and Female Leaders?" *Academy of Management Journal* 60, no. 2
(2017): 771–797; Sharon Mavin, "Queen Bees, Wannabees, and Afraid
to Bees: No More 'Best Enemies' for Women in Management?" *British
Journal of Management* 19 (2008): S75–S84.

4. Klea Faniko, Naomi Ellemers, and Belle Derks, "The Queen
Bee Phenomenon in Academia 15 Years After: Does It Still Exist,
and If So, Why?" *British Journal of Social Psychology* 60, no. 2 (2021):
383–399; Annika Scholl et al., "Highly Identified Power-Holders
Feel Responsible: The Interplay Between Social Identification and
Social Power Within Groups," *British Journal of Social Psychology* 57,
no. 1 (2018): 112–129; Michelle M. Duguid, Denise Lewin
Loyd, and Pamela S. Tolbert, "The Impact of Categorical Status,
Numeric Representation, and Work Group Prestige on Preference
for Demographically Similar Others: A Value Threat Approach,"
Organization Science 23, no. 2 (2012): 386–401.

5. Joan C. Williams, Rachel Korn, and Rachel Maas, "The Elephant in
the (Well-Designed) Room: An Investigation into Bias in the Architecture
Profession," The Center for WorkLife Law, forthcoming 2021, 96.

6. Prithviraj Chattopadhyay, Malgorzata Tluchowska, and Elizabeth George, "Identifying the Ingroup: A Closer Look at the Influence of Demographic Dissimilarity on Employee Social Identity," *Academy of Management Review* 29, no. 2 (2004): 180–202; Susanah Lily L. Mendoza, *Between the Homeland and the Diaspora: The Politics of Theorizing Filipino and Filipino American Identities: A Second Look at the Poststructuralism-Indigenization Debates* (London: Psychology Press, 2002); Naomi Ellemers et al., "The Underrepresentation of Women in Science: Differential Commitment or the Queen Bee Syndrome?" *British Journal of Social Psychology* 43, no. 3 (2004): 315–338; Leah D. Sheppard and Karl Aquino, "Much Ado About Nothing? Observers' Problematization of Women's Same-Sex Conflict at Work," *Academy of Management Perspectives* 27, no. 1 (2013): 52–62; Robin J. Ely, "The Effects of Organizational Demographics and Social Identity on Relationships Among Professional Women," *Administrative Science Quarterly* (1994): 203–238.

7. Twymon v. Wells Fargo & Co., 462 F.3d 925, 936 (8th Cir. 2006).

8. Ibid., at 931.

9. Belle Derks et al., "Gender-Bias Primes Elicit Queen-Bee Responses Among Senior Policewomen," *Psychological Science* 22, no. 10 (2011): 1243–1249; Klea Faniko, Naomi Ellemers, and Belle Derks, "The Queen Bee Phenomenon in Academia 15 Years After"; Belle Derks et al., "Do Sexist Organizational Cultures Create the Queen Bee?" *British Journal of Social Psychology* 50, no. 3 (2011): 519–535.

10. Leah D. Sheppard and Karl Aquino, "Much Ado About Nothing?"

11. Joan C. Williams, Katherine W. Phillips, and Erika V. Hall, "Double Jeopardy? Gender Bias Against Women of Color in Science," The Center for WorkLife Law, 2015, https://worklifelaw.org /publications/Double-Jeopardy-Report_v6_full_web-sm.pdf.

12. Felice Batlan, "'If You Become His Second Wife, You Are a Fool': Shifting Paradigms of the Roles, Perceptions, and Working Conditions of Legal Secretaries in Large Law Firms," in *Special Issue: Law Firms, Legal Culture, and Legal Practice*, ed. Austin Sarat (Bingley, UK: Emerald Group Publishing Limited, 2010), 169–210.

13. Ibid.

14. Joan C. Williams, Katherine W. Phillips, and Erika V. Hall, "Double Jeopardy?"

15. Ibid.

16. Stephanie K. Johnson and David R. Hekman, "Women and Minorities Are Penalized for Promoting Diversity"; David R. Hekman

et al., "Does Diversity-Valuing Behavior Result in Diminished Performance Ratings for Non-White and Female Leaders?"; Sharon Mavin, "Queen Bees, Wannabees, and Afraid to Bees: No More 'Best Enemies' for Women in Management?"

Chapter 11

1. Rik Kirkland and Iris Bohnet, "Focusing on What Works for Workplace Diversity," McKinsey & Company, April 7, 2017, https://www.mckinsey.com/featured-insights/gender-equality/focusing-on-what-works-for-workplace-diversity.

2. Frank Dobbin, Daniel Schrage, and Alexandra Kalev, "Rage Against the Iron Cage: The Varied Effects of Bureaucratic Personnel Reforms on Diversity," *American Sociological Review* 80, no. 5 (2015): 1014–1044; Alexandra Kalev, Frank Dobbin, and Erin Kelly, "Best Practices or Best Guesses? Assessing the Efficacy of Corporate Affirmative Action and Diversity Policies," *American Sociological Review* 71, no. 4 (2006): 589–617.

3. Ibid.

4. Katherine W. Phillips, "How Diversity Makes Us Smarter," *Scientific American*, October 1, 2014, https://doi.org/10.1038/scientificamerican1014-42.

5. Steve Lohr, "Facial Recognition Is Accurate, If You're a White Guy," *New York Times*, February 9, 2018, https://www.nytimes.com/2018/02/09/technology/facial-recognition-race-artificial-intelligence.html; James Vincent, "Google 'Fixed' Its Racist Algorithm by Removing Gorillas from Its Image-Labeling Tech," The Verge, January 12, 2018, https://www.theverge.com/2018/1/12/16882408/google-racist-gorillas-photo-recognition-algorithm-ai.

6. Cristina Díaz-García, Angela González-Moreno, and Francisco Jose Sáez-Martínez, "Gender Diversity within R&D Teams: Its Impact on Radicalness of Innovation," *Innovation* 15, no. 2 (2013): 149–160.

7. Alexandra Kalev and Frank Dobbin, "Does Diversity Training Increase Corporate Diversity? Regulation Backlash and Regulatory Accountability," working paper, Mossavar-Rahmani Center For Business and Government, Harvard Kennedy School, https://scholar.harvard.edu/files/dobbin/files/dobbin_-_aatraining_clean.pdf.

8. Ibid.; Alexandra Kalev, Frank Dobbin, and Erin Kelly, "Best Practices or Best Guesses?"

9. Paul Gompers and Silpa Kovvali, "The Other Diversity Dividend," *Harvard Business Review*, July–August 2018.

10. Sheen S. Levine et al., "Ethnic Diversity Deflates Price Bubbles," *Proceedings of the National Academy of Sciences* 111, no. 52 (2014): 18524–18529.

11. Katherine W. Phillips, "How Diversity Makes Us Smarter."

12. Deborah L. Kidder et al., "Backlash Toward Diversity Initiatives: Examining the Impact of Diversity Program Justification, Personal and Group Outcomes," *International Journal of Conflict Management* 15, no. 1 (2004): 77–102.

13. Vivian Hunt, Dennis Layton, and Sara Prince, "Why Diversity Matters," McKinsey & Company, January 1, 2015, https://www.mckinsey.com/business-functions/organization/our-insights/why-diversity-matters.

14. Cedric Herring, "Does Diversity Pay? Race, Gender, and the Business Case for Diversity," *American Sociological Review* 74, no. 2 (2009): 208–224.

15. Katherine W. Phillips, "How Diversity Makes Us Smarter."

16. John P. Kotter, "Leading Change: Why Transformation Efforts Fail," *Harvard Business Review*, May–June 1995, https://hbr.org/1995/05/leading-change-why-transformation-efforts-fail-2.

17. Joan C. Williams, "Keeping Diversity Metrics While Controlling for Legal Risk," The Center for WorkLife Law, https://www.biasinterrupters.org.

18. John P. Kotter, "Leading Change."

19. Alexandra Kalev and Frank Dobbin, "Does Diversity Training Increase Corporate Diversity?"

20. John P. Kotter, "Leading Change."

Chapter 12

1. Joan C. Williams, Rachel Korn, and Rachel Maas, "Pinning Down the Jellyfish: Women of Color in Tech," The Center for WorkLife Law, forthcoming 2021.

2. Joan C. Williams and Sky Mihaylo, "How the Best Bosses Interrupt Bias on Their Teams," *Harvard Business Review,* November–December 2019.

3. Joan C. Williams and James D. White, "Update Your DE&I Playbook," hbr.org, July 15, 2020, https://hbr.org/2020/07/update-your-dei-playbook.

4. Jennifer S. Lerner and Philip E. Tetlock, "Accounting for the Effects of Accountability," *Psychological Bulletin* 125, no. 2 (1999): 255–275.

5. Stephanie K. Johnson and David R. Hekman, "Women and Minorities Are Penalized for Promoting Diversity," *Harvard Business Review*, March 23, 2016, https://hbr.org/2016/03/women-and -minorities-are-penalized-for-promoting-diversity; David R. Hekman et al., "Does Diversity-Valuing Behavior Result in Diminished Performance Ratings for Non-White and Female Leaders?" *Academy of Management Journal* 60, no. 2 (2017): 771–797; Sharon Mavin, "Queen Bees, Wannabees, and Afraid to Bees: No More 'Best Enemies' for Women in Management?" *British Journal of Management* 19 (2008): S75–S84.

6. Ronald S. Burt, *Structural Holes* (Boston: Harvard University Press, 1992), 74–75, 161, 165.

7. Alexandra Kalev, Frank Dobbin, and Erin Kelly, "Best Practices or Best Guesses? Assessing the Efficacy of Corporate Affirmative Action and Diversity Policies," *American Sociological Review* 71, no. 4 (2006): 589–617.

8. Frank Dobbin, "Do Faculty Diversity Programs Work?: Evidence from 600 Universities, 1993–2015," Presentation at the Dutch Network of Women Professors (LNVH) Women Professors Monitor 2019, Nieuwspoort, The Hague, December 12, 2019.

Chapter 13

1. Herminia Ibarra, Robin J. Ely, and Deborah M. Kolb, "Women Rising: The Unseen Barriers," *Harvard Business Review,* September 2013.

Chapter 14

1. Riley Newman and Elena Grewal, "Beginning with Ourselves," Medium, February 18, 2016, https://medium.com/airbnb-engineering /beginning-with-ourselves-48c5ed46a703.

2. Stephanie K. Johnson, David R. Hekman, and Elsa T. Chan, "If There's Only One Woman in Your Candidate Pool, There's Statistically No Chance She'll Be Hired," hbr.org, April 26, 2016, https://hbr .org/2016/04/if-theres-only-one-woman-in-your-candidate-pool -theres-statistically-no-chance-shell-be-hired.

3. Frank Dobbin, Daniel Schrage, and Alexandra Kalev, "Rage Against the Iron Cage: The Varied Effects of Bureaucratic Personnel Reforms on Diversity," *American Sociological Review* 80, no. 5 (2015): 1014–1044.

4. Stacy Dale and Alan B. Krueger, "Estimating the Return to College Selectivity Over the Career Using Administrative Earnings Data," working paper 17159, National Bureau of Economic Research, 2011.

5. Tanja Hentschel et al., "Sounds Like a Fit! Wording in Recruitment Advertisements and Recruiter Gender Affect Women's Pursuit of Career Development Programs via Anticipated Belongingness," *Human Resource Management* (2020): 1–22; LinkedIn, "Language Matters: How Words Impact Men and Women in the Workplace," 2019 https://business.linkedin.com/content/dam/me /business/en-us/talent-solutions-lodestone/body/pdf/Linkedin -Language-Matters-Report-FINAL2.pdf; ZipRecruiter, "Removing These Gendered Keywords Gets You More Applicants," ZipRecruiter blog, September 19, 2016, https://www.ziprecruiter.com/blog /removing-gendered-keywords-gets-you-more-applicants/; Danielle Gaucher, Justin Friesen, and Aaron C. Kay, "Evidence That Gendered Wording in Job Advertisements Exists and Sustains Gender Inequality," *Journal of Personality and Social Psychology* 101, no. 1 (March 2011): 109–128.

6. Andreas Leibbrandt and John A. List, "Do Women Avoid Salary Negotiations? Evidence from a Large-Scale Natural Field Experiment," *Management Science* 61, no. 9 (2015): 2016–2024.

7. Linda Babcock, H. Bowles, and Julia Bear, "A Model of When to Negotiate," in *The Oxford Handbook of Economic Conflict Resolution*, eds. Rachel Croson and Gary E. Bolton (Oxford University Press, 2012): 313–331.

8. Laszlo Bock, *Work Rules!* (New York: Twelve, 2015), 12; Warren Thorngate, Robyn M. Dawes, and Margaret Foddy, *Judging Merit* (London: Psychology Press, 2010).

9. Joni Hersch, "Opting Out Among Women with Elite Education," *Review of Economics of the Household* 11, no. 4 (2013): 469–506.

10. Warren Thorngate, Robyn M. Dawes, and Margaret Foddy, *Judging Merit*.

11. Laszlo Bock, *Work Rules!*

12. Pascaline Dupas et al., "Gender and the Dynamics of Economics Seminars," working paper 28494, National Bureau of Economic Research, 2021.

13. Lily Jampol and Vivian Zayas, "Gendered White Lies: Women Are Given Inflated Performance Feedback Compared with Men," *Personality and Social Psychology Bulletin* 47, no. 1 (2021): 57–69.

14. Ibid.

Chapter 15

1. Katherine W. Phillips, "How Diversity Makes Us Smarter," *Scientific American*, October 1, 2014, https://doi.org/10.1038/scientificamerican1014-42.

2. Anita Williams Woolley et al., "Evidence for a Collective Intelligence Factor in the Performance of Human Groups," *Science* 330, no. 6004 (2010): 686–688; Anita Williams Woolley, Ishani Aggarwal, and Thomas W. Malone, "Collective Intelligence and Group Performance," *Current Directions in Psychological Science* 24, no. 6 (2015): 420–424; Julia Bear and Anita Williams Woolley, "The Role of Gender in Team Collaboration and Performance," *Interdisciplinary Science Reviews* 36, no. 2 (2011): 146–153.

3. Samuel R. Sommers, "On Racial Diversity and Group Decision Making: Identifying Multiple Effects of Racial Composition on Jury Deliberations," *Journal of Personality and Social Psychology* 90, no. 4 (2006): 597–612.

4. Anthony Lising Antonio et al., "Effects of Racial Diversity on Complex Thinking in College Students," *Psychological Science* 15, no. 8 (2004): 507–510.

5. Katherine W. Phillips, Katie A. Liljenquist, and Margaret A. Neale, "Is the Pain Worth the Gain? The Advantages and Liabilities of Agreeing with Socially Distinct Newcomers," *Personality and Social Psychology Bulletin* 35, no. 3 (2009): 336–350.

6. Stephanie K. Johnson and David R. Hekman, "Women and Minorities Are Penalized for Promoting Diversity," hbr.org, March 23, 2016, https://hbr.org/2016/03/women-and-minorities-are-penalized-for-promoting-diversity; David R. Hekman et al., "Does Diversity-Valuing Behavior Result in Diminished Performance Ratings for Non-White and Female Leaders?" *Academy of Management Journal* 60, no. 2 (2017): 771–797; Sharon Mavin, "Queen Bees, Wannabees, and Afraid to Bees: No More 'Best Enemies' for Women in Management?" *British Journal of Management* 19 (2008): S75–S84.

7. Melissa C. Thomas-Hunt and Katherine W. Phillips, "When What You Know Is Not Enough: Expertise and Gender Dynamics in Task Groups," *Personality and Social Psychology Bulletin* 30, no. 12 (2004): 1585–1598.

8. Christopher F. Karpowitz, Tali Mendelberg, and Lee Shaker, "Gender Inequality in Deliberative Participation," *American Political Science Review* (2012): 533–547.

9. Cecilia L. Ridgeway and Joseph Berger, "Expectations, Legitimation, and Dominance Behavior in Task Groups," *American Sociological Review* (1986): 603–617.

10. Data generated by Rachel Korn, Director of Research on Organization Bias at WorkLife Law, based on the US Census Bureau's American Community Survey, 2021, https://data.census.gov/cedsci.

11. PwC, "Millennials at Work: Reshaping the Workplace," 2011, 1–28.

12. PwC, "It's Time to Reimagine Where and How Work Will Get Done," PwC's US Remote Work Survey, January 12, 2021, https://www.pwc.com/us/en/library/covid-19/us-remote-work-survey.html.

13. Jack Zenger and Joseph Folkman, "The Ideal Praise-to-Criticism Ratio," hbr.org, March 15, 2013, https://hbr.org/2013/03/the-ideal-praise-to-criticism.

14. Shankar Vedantam, "A Creature of Habit," *Hidden Brain*, podcast, December 28, 2020.

15. Shelley J. Correll and Caroline Simard, "Research: Vague Feedback Is Holding Women Back," hbr.org, April 29, 2016, https://hbr.org/2016/04/research-vague-feedback-is-holding-women-back; Lily Jampol and Vivian Zayas, "Gendered White Lies: Women Are Given Inflated Performance Feedback Compared with Men," *Personality and Social Psychology Bulletin* 47, no. 1 (2021): 57–69; Stacy Blake-Beard, "Mentoring: Creating Mutually Empowering Relationships," Clayman Institute, YouTube video, https://www.youtube.com/watch?v=7HumPsn83RE.

16. Lily Jampol and Vivian Zayas, "Gendered White Lies."

17. Joan C. Williams et al., "You Can't Change What You Can't See: Interrupting Racial and Gender Bias in the Legal Profession," American Bar Association and Minority Corporate Counsel Association, 2018, 24; Joan C. Williams, Katherine W. Phillips, and Erika V. Hall, "Double Jeopardy? Gender Bias Against Women of Color in Science," The Center for WorkLife Law, 2015, 18, https://worklifelaw.org/publications/Double-Jeopardy-Report_v6_full_web-sm.pdf.

Conclusion

1. Shankar Vedantam, "Radically Normal: How Gay Rights Activists Changed the Minds of Their Opponents,"*Hidden Brain*, podcast, April 8, 2019.

INDEX

Note: The letter *f* following a page number denotes a figure.

ACKNOWLEDGMENTS

Every book is the product of community, and this one is no exception.

This book would not have been possible without the work of everyone who helped develop the Workplace Experiences Survey. The idea was Erika Hall's when she was just a graduate student (she's now a business school professor at Emory), and I hired her to help me with the report "Double Jeopardy? Gender Bias against Women of Color in STEM." She suggested adding a survey, which we did using lines of questioning I had developed in the interviews of my book *What Works for Women at Work*. I am eternally grateful to her, and to Kathy Phillips, who referred me to Erika and helped us with "Double Jeopardy?" Kathy's untimely death in 2020 leaves us bereft of both a powerful scholar and a powerful spirit.

Professor Rich Lee also provided crucial help when we decided to add questions about racial stereotypes, given his expertise on Asian Americans.

Rachel Korn and Su Li, successive research directors at WorkLife Law, took the laboring oar in producing all the survey data presented here. They have been very patient with me!

When I wrote *What Works for Women at Work*, I had given up on the possibility of organizational change. I owe bias interrupters to Sarah Green Carmichael, my longtime editor at *Harvard Business Review* (now at Bloomberg), who insisted that I write an organizational change piece based on *What Works for Women at Work*. That became "Hacking Tech's Diversity Problem," edited by Sarah and published in HBR in 2014. Sarah also taught me the question-and-answer format of this book when she edited my last book, *White Working Class*. She edited this one, too, because I can't imagine writing a book without her.

I was equally lucky with my HBR Press editor this time, Scott Berinato, whose expertise in the graphical display of information was a truly invaluable contribution. Scott, my thanks to you for completely transforming the way I communicate complex data sets. You helped me express in stunningly simple terms something I have been trying to express for over a decade: how white men's experiences differ from those of every other group. And thanks for the editing, too!

Two of my board members, Elvir Causevic and Amber Lee Williams, both read through the entire manuscript and gave invaluable suggestions. Another board member, Laura Maechtlen, made important contributions to chapter 12. My colleague Shauna Marshall made important contributions to chapter 10, and more generally to my understanding of race in America. My friend of half a century, Nino Magliocco, also contributed his experience as a CEO—as did Elvir.

This book would not even have been remotely possible without my amazing research librarian Hilary Hardcastle.

Nor would it have been without my team at WorkLife Law. Rachel Korn, our research director, is responsible for leading many of the studies based on the Workplace Experiences Survey, and for providing the quantitative expertise I lack. Mikayla Boginsky worked tirelessly with her usual phenomenal dedication and efficiency to get this manuscript out the door, aided by Joahna Cervantes. Julia Crawford worked for weeks scrubbing the footnotes. The remainder of the team at WorkLife Law—Chelsey Crowley, Jamie Dolkas, Juliana Franco, Jessica Lee, and Liz Morris—kept things cooking while I was busy in another kitchen, as did Cynthia Thomas Calvert, my partner in crime for over twenty years.

Most of all I want to thank my family. My son, Nick Williams, defended his dissertation in the middle of this book's writing, making him the first Dr. Williams in the history of our family. My daughter, Rachel Dempsey, with whom I wrote *What Works for Women at Work*, taught me most of what I know about how to write for a popular audience. My husband of forty-three years, James X. Dempsey, is my rock: he cheers me up when social inequality gets me down. I love them all very much.

ABOUT THE AUTHOR

JOAN C. WILLIAMS is a Distinguished Professor of Law, Hastings Foundation Chair, and Founding Director of the Center for WorkLife Law at the University of California, Hastings College of the Law. Described as having "something approaching rock star status" in her field by the *New York Times Magazine*, she has played a central role in reshaping the conversation about work and workplace bias over the past quarter century. Williams has authored 12 books and 115 academic articles, and she is the eleventh-most-cited scholar in her field. Her best-known prior books are *White Working Class* and *What Works for Women at Work*, coauthored with her daughter, Rachel Dempsey, and now in its tenth edition.

Williams has been on the forefront of research focused on how gender and racial bias play out in everyday workplace interactions for more than two decades and has coauthored a series of influential reports on workplace bias in engineering, academia, tech, architecture, and the legal profession. She is widely known for "bias interrupters," an evidence-based, metrics-driven approach to eradicating implicit bias, which was introduced in the *Harvard Business Review* in 2014. The website www.biasinterrupters.org, with open-source tool kits for individuals and organizations, has been accessed more than 240,000 times from around the world and has been so influential in Europe that Williams was awarded an honorary PhD from Utrecht University in 2018.

Williams' work is well-known among business leaders, HR professionals, and individuals. She has published thirty articles in *Harvard Business Review*, including one of the most-read articles in its one hundred-year history. Her TED talk, "Why Corporate Diversity Programs Fail—and How Small Tweaks Can Have a Big Impact," has been viewed more than one million times, and videos she created for LeanIn.org about *What Works. for Women at Work* were featured on Virgin Airlines as in-flight entertainment, seen literally around the world.

Awards include the Society of Women Engineers' President's Award (2019), the Families and Work Institute's Work Life Legacy Award (2014), the American Bar Foundation's Outstanding Scholar Award (2012), the American Bar Association's Margaret Brent Award for Women Lawyers of Achievement (2006), and the Distinguished Publication Award of the Association for Women in Psychology (2004; with Monica Biernat and Faye Crosby). In 2008, she gave the William E. Massey Sr. Lectures in the History of American Civilization at Harvard.

Williams obtained a BA in history from Yale University, a master's degree in city planning from Massachusetts Institute of Technology, and a JD from Harvard Law School. She resides in San Francisco with her husband, James X. Dempsey. She enjoys hiking, making jam, and spending time with her children, Rachel Dempsey and Nick Williams.